"Finally, a book that called me beyond mission. Different captures God's deep heart for transforming the world through the transformed saint and sinner. This is a rare and legit read if you plan to follow Jesus anytime soon."

HUGH HALTER
Author of The Tangible Kingdom and FLESH

"In Different, Mike Patz and Brian Sanders show that holiness is essential to the nature of discipleship and provides us with an alternative story to the predominant story of the world around about us—it is essential to our relationship with God as well as our witness in the world. Well formulated, uncompromisingly radical, yet grounded in real life, this book is an essential corrective to the spiritual malaise of the contemporary church."

ALAN HIRSCH
Author of The Forgotten Ways and The Shaping of Things To Come, and coauthor of The Permanent Revolution

"A needed call to be other than, but part of, the world. Mike and Brian are word smiths, but without being "cute." They get to the point but with a wonderful turn of phase that causes one to laugh and cry—sometimes in the same few moments. I am moved by Different. Together, the two have discovered a voice that needs to be heard. They write with clarity. They issue a thoughtful, deep call to a historically rooted yet profoundly needed discipleship. Their book proves again that the radical middle is not mushy or compromised."

FLOYD MCCLUNG
Author, founder and international director of All Nations

"The title for this book really does say it all. It's a truly different approach to how the church views holiness in the context of our mission as disciples. The irony is, there's nothing new or radical here, except for the fact that "Different" calls us back to scripture, to the face of God, and to the things that made the church revolutionary in the first century. But it's not a stroll down memory lane and it doesn't idolize the past or swoon with nostalgia for the days when America was a "Christian nation." It is extremely practical because it's so Biblical. Moreover, I have seen the principles in these pages lived out in the real context of a real church that reaches real sinners and disciples and sends out real servants on mission. Without hesitation I encourage you to move this book to now" list. It's a true gift to the bo

CLAYTON KING
Founder and President, C Ministries
Teaching Pastor, NewSpring rsity

different

REIMAGINING HOLINESS FOR A WANDERING CHURCH IN A WATCHING WORLD

MIKE PATZ &
BRIAN SANDERS

differentbook.org

Published by Underground Media
1925 E 2nd Avenue
Tampa, FL 33605
www.undergroundglobal.com
©2014 Underground Media

Design: Jessie Rajski

ISBN 978-0-9845758-6-2

Printed in the United States

For our spiritual families,
Greenhouse and Underground—
and all those disciples who embody the
sacrifice and difference we have tried to
describe here, for being the holy fuel
that God has used to inspire us
and renew our hope.

TABLE OF CONTENTS

ONE

TWO
THREE
FOUR
FIVE
SIX
SEVEN
EIGHT
NINE
TEN
ELEVEN
TWELVE

Indifference, Aliens, and Contextualized Holiness

You never change the world by being just like it. Change requires something different. We think that is holiness. The questions being asked from both inside and outside the church will have no meaningful answers if we are not holy as he is holy. But what does it really mean to be Holy?

Elie Wiesel famously wrote that the opposite of love is not hate, it is indifference.[1] Drawing from his childhood experience in a Nazi concentration camp, it was not the wicked hostility of a fascist regime that he found most unlike God, but the apathy of a population of average people who agreed silently to the atrocities while saying and doing nothing. The opposite of love is not hate; it is doing nothing in the face of hate. It is going along and being the same.

When we consider the church of Jesus, the message of scripture, the good news of the kingdom, and the mission of God in the world, we are confronted with an immeasurably weighty subject. We are confronted with a responsibility that is both profound and eternal and a God that is worthy of all that we have and more. Yet, when we look at the western churches that we learn in—and even lead—we are shaken by the lack of those qualities in the people who have supposedly accepted that responsibly. In a sense, we come from a church that is different in the wrong way. We are different from the call of scripture and the cruciform life we see in its pages. Disciples of Jesus and the churches they form are meant to stand out from the patterns of this world and its hatreds. Yet too often in our assessment, we are not different.

The Latin etymology of the word *indifference* is simply "to be want of difference, to be similar." In our minds, the church is want of difference. We are in need of difference, and the indifferent Christians and communities we have formed have wronged the world in a way that may be even greater than hatred because we have not even cared. "Would that you were hot or cold, but because you are luke warm..."[2]

Maybe spiritual apathy—and indifference in the common sense of the word—comes from a lack of distinction and conviction. Maybe the church is not what it could be because we have not loved our world enough to stand out in it. We wonder if the attempt to reach and walk alongside the world has left our unbelieving friends no clarity on how to believe or where to go from where they are. If we are not different, then what is conversion? If we are not different, then what does repentance mean? If we are not different, then what is regeneration, sanctification, freedom, healing, and wholeness? If we are not different and if the kingdom of God is just going and sitting at the same bar stool with the same people, then what does it mean to enter it?

We are convinced that passionate love for God and the world he came to save will produce disciples who stand with, but not as, the lost world. We can walk alongside people and still stand out from them. Disciples cannot call other disciples to repentance and change if they are not themselves changed and changing. Churches cannot serve their divine purpose to call cities and systems to redemption and change if they are not themselves redeemed and redemptive.

When we argue that the church should be different from the world we don't mean to conjure some prudish, cliché impression of Christians handling snakes, preaching with a bullhorn, or storing canned goods in the basement for Armageddon. There are ways that Christians have, on occasion, stood out that were neither loving nor redemptive. We are not making a call to the church to be alienated or disconnected from real people in the real world. We believe in ministry that is incarnational, that is relevant, that is modern; but it has to be done by people who are fundamentally different from those they are looking to love. There has to be a noteworthy distinction that is both meaningful and desirable. Our marriages should last longer, our kids more secure, our integrity more certain, our lives more interesting, and our relationship with God plain to see.

TO FEEL OR NOT TO FEEL

There is a lingering legacy of the ancient ideological struggle between the Stoics and the Epicureans. Like all enduring debates, it continues because it is still a real dilemma for people. And, as is often the case, Jesus offers us a third way, affirming and challenging the notions of both groups.

For the Stoics the goal of life was *apathia*, or a life without the suffering of emotion. Pathos was seen as weak and unpredictable, and even God comes to be seen as apathetic. In modern English to call someone pathetic is to level an almost debilitating insult to their person and to their individuality. We call people pathetic when we think their emotion has made them completely impotent. Emotion is weak.

On the other side of the debate, the Epicureans favored a life of passion and saying yes to desire. However, giving in to passion and emotion may exult us into momentary ecstasy that leaves us hung over and struggling to pick up the moral and relational pieces of our lives the next morning. Apathy or Passion? Where does Jesus lead us?

Apathia as an objection to ungoverned passion is correct in its critique but wrong in its application. The solution to emotionalism is not apathy, it is sacrificial love. Jesus shows us a God who is empathetic, compassionate and who loves with an indomitable force, revealing the strength of emotion that finds its origin in the heart of God. We are made to be passionate. To love and live life as if it were a joy and an adventure. However, that kind of passion is really only possible when we anchor it in the will and way of God. Indifference has come to mean apathy because we have lost the will to love. If we make a call to the people of God to be different, that call has to be rooted in love. Love for Jesus and love for people.

Both Stoics and Epicureans shared a desire to rid their lives of suffering. The goal of *apathia* was not to suffer the pain of emotion. Likewise, the goal of the hedonist was to embrace desire in the avoidance of pain and suffering. Jesus' way reveals a people who are passionate, but that passion does not come from our desire to avoid pain. On the contrary, we love so deeply that we are ready to suffer for that love. This is the way of Jesus.

As N.T. Wright explains, "One of the central elements of the Christian story is the claim that the paradox of laughter and tears, woven as it is deep into the heart of all human experience, is woven also deep into the heart of God." We embrace both celebration and sorrow because we hear the music and dance to both the dirge and the jig. This is what makes us different. We embrace passion mitigated by the discipline and guidance of love.

A HOPEFUL TURN

This book is meant as a prophetic invitation to love by standing out. It is meant to be a treatise against spiritual apathy and indifference. And it is meant to be a vision for what disciples and the church can be when it is mobilized, motivated, and calibrated for redemption and not assimilation. It is meant as a theology of protest against concessions to evil in our world and even our churches. It is meant to be a handbook for discipleship in a new kind of church, one that is new in its sensibilities but very old in its identity. It is an invitation to be different.

For years both of us worked under other leaders with a vision and a style of church that was there before we came. We are eternally grateful for solid leaders who loved Jesus and led us well. In both our cases, we were fortunate to work with great people and to be part of growing ministries. Still, we never really fully believed in the structures and choices of the institutions we inherited. They were great people in lousy systems, and our experiences left us with a sense of the inadequacies of church life. We both felt this inevitable kind of disappointment, that what we saw in the pages of the New Testament was not what we saw in our communities. Even more, there seemed to be an unspoken consensus among people who had done ministry longer than us that settling was simply part of ministry life.

The second half of our ministry careers have seen us shift into the primary leadership roles of the communities we serve. Mike became a Senior Pastor, and Brian started an entirely new nonprofit. After some time leading our own communities, we are moved to report that this settling isn't the required case. The church is not a myth. We are tired of telling people worn out and fed up with their church to just hang in there. We are tired of settling. We have come to realize that imperfect churches can still be breathtaking churches, and that imperfect disciples can still turn heads, inspire, and remind everyone they meet of the God-man Jesus. Our communities, while starting from two very different points, have converged on a kind of *esprit de corps* that can only be attributed to the work of Holy Spirit. If you talk to almost anyone associated with Mike's church or Brian's network, they will tell you the same story, and words will fail them as they try to describe the thing that God is doing.

Part of our intention behind this book is to tell that story, not in a narrative sense but in a principled sense. We want to catalog and memorialize the commitments and convictions of our communities. We are not so self-involved as to believe that our stories are wholly unique. We know that many of our readers will recognize their own communities in these principles. But many others will not, and our hope is to stir a holy jealously for the church to have the kind of creativity, joy, and effectiveness we have witnessed. We don't have to settle for less, but it will require that we be willing to be different.

HOLINESS REVISITED

At least at the time of writing, we find there is precious little currently being written and read about holiness. An n-gram view of the word's usage in the history of modern literature shows a steep and steady decline at the turn of the 20th century with virtually no change to today. It simply isn't a popular word in our contemporary lexicon. Even in Christian circles, it doesn't seem like a contemporary missional or ecclesial concept. Still, holiness, so paramount to the description of God, and in turn, so crucial to the identification of the people of God, is a necessary biblical concept. Jesus said we ought to be holy, in the same way that the Father is holy.[3] Presumably in the same way that he was holy. In essence, what is holiness if not positive difference? The invitation to be different then is an invitation to holiness. It is an invitation to discover the character and nature of God and then to try and imitate that character both in our own lives and the constitution of our collective lives together.

Holiness has come to mean a kind of pedantic legalism (not drinking or smoking), yet those distinctions were nevertheless an attempt to set the people of God apart from the rest of the world. We applaud that impulse, if not the application. In fact, with the growing movement of young Christians rediscovering mission, this impulse has become indispensable again. Without incarnation and real relationship with the unbelieving world, there can be no mission. Amen. But without holiness there can be no effect to the mission we do.

We may be learning again to be missional (and our communities are at the vanguard in this regard), but it does not mean that the mission we do is actually working. We have learned to move back into the inner city, find the third places, recapture the workplace as a legitimate mission context, and rightly redefine the missionary to be *any* follower of Jesus, not just paid clergy, but it does not mean that our missionary work is actually effective. We should ask, has our relocation and recalibration to mission actually had any effect?

So many of our friends are motivated by the idea of church planting, but if the churches we plant do not transform the places we plant them, how is that an ultimate goal? Planting churches is fine if what is planted brings the kingdom of God and its righteousness with it.

We can say, being very close to this movement, that it is not enough to inhabit (incarnate) the pub if there is no visible and audible witness, and even more poignantly, if there is no discernible holiness of the witness herself.

Given the recent history of the church moving away from mission and embracing the teaching and pastoral gifts while neglecting the apostolic, prophetic, and evangelistic ones, it is not hard to see why we cheer and celebrate as heroes those among us who have "pitched their tents" alongside the lost and the poor. We are a part of that groundswell toward incarnation and mission, but that simply is not enough. It is like we are cheering on the team for putting on their uniforms. I suppose, being out of the game so long, it might give some cause for celebration, but it does not mean that we've even begun to play, and it certainly doesn't mean that we've won.

Although it might still seem like a new message for some, we are 10 years into that truth, and we grow tired of the church cheering for people who "step out" or "take a risk." That is the first step, but a decade of stepping out and taking risks has left us wanting more. In that initial rediscovery, there is the sense that ministry is adventure, but a decade later we are beginning to understand that ministry is more like art. It might be an adventure to paint your first portrait or write your first poem, but after years of painting and writing you begin to chase proficiency, dreaming for a masterpiece.

Holiness is the biblical concept we chase. To be different in the way that God is different. Not to be transcendent, but to embody transcendence. To live in a way that boggles the minds of onlookers, that provokes the soul to jealousy, and that fascinates the heart.

We want to identify what sets us apart and how to be truly holy. We want to identify what it looks, smells, feels, and tastes like to be holy. We have written this book to respond to 12 provocative questions posed in Scripture. They are questions that invite us to consider our relationship with God and in turn, our relationship with the world we live in. They are questions with implications for every individual Christian and the churches we form together. We mean for this book to be a survey of what we believe, values for a relevant and potent contextualization of the church in our time. Still, there are plenty of things missing. While these 12 themes represent critical issues for us to understand and embody, that does not mean that other biblical themes are somehow less important. These are simply the questions we believe most need to be asked (and answered) right now, and it is our heartfelt conviction that Christians who can live in the biblical call that these themes unearth will change the world.

SPIRITUAL STOCKHOLM SYNDROME

In August 1973, a bank was robbed in Stockholm, Sweden, resulting in a six-day hostage crisis. Several bank employees were held in the vault as their captors found themselves in a stand-off with police. What is both remarkable and memorable about this robbery was the reaction of the hostages. The captives spent so much time in the orbit of these robbers they became emotionally attached to them, becoming more and more sympathetic to their cause. Refusing help from the police, the victims actually defended their captors when the ordeal was over. They had come to see the criminals as their friends and their saviors as their enemies. From this episode the term Stockholm Syndrome was coined to refer to the phenomenon of captives sympathizing and even taking the side of their kidnappers.

We all suffer from a kind of spiritual Stockholm Syndrome. Our sympathy is given to whoever is closest to us. When that is Jesus, we are freed to live a life of loving protest against the things and people that would enslave us. However, when we are closer to our captors than we are to Jesus, we begin to sympathize with them, their rationale, and their motivations. We are captives but begin to forget that we are. We begin to love the world that hates us and hate the God who loves us. We get it all backwards.

Maybe we have to love our world by saying no to it, by walking away, by calling it to account, and by offering it a prophetic challenge. We forgive because we first recognize that something is sin. We believe in redemption because we believe in judgment. We can offer mercy because we, of all the people in the earth, understand justice. But this is only possible if we are more deeply connected to Jesus than we are to our context, when we are loved more by Jesus than by the world. When the church has come to that conviction it has often (erroneously) concluded that it must therefore withdraw from the world in order to deny its influence. Declining participation in something doesn't lessen its influence; in many cases, it only deepens it. Just ask the desert Fathers, whose retreat to the wilderness was most often characterized not with intimacy with God but with an encounter with the Devil. The desert is not the answer for holiness, and it is certainly not the answer for mission. We have to search for a middle ground in delivering a holy life in the midst of the world we live in. We have to find a way to contextualize holiness.

NEW HOLINESS

Clearly, the word doesn't make the list of Christianity's most popular terms these days. That's because we forgot what it means. But we need our word back and these chapters are an effort to recapture the raw beauty and untamed power of this thing we call holiness.

The word itself carries the thought of being separated *from* one thing... and set apart *for* some other thing. *For* God. *For* a unique purpose. Holy. *Different*. Consider that word, and just how hard it can be to embody.

Ever since the Fall, humans have had this desire to fit, to belong, to be on the *inside* of some cosmic location that we can't quite put our finger on. We just know we're on the outside, and nobody wants to be alienated.

I (Mike) remember this feeling as a child when our family moved, and I was forced into a new school. I'm not sure if it had more to do with beginning middle school or the realization that my classmates were more affluent than we were, but I soon felt the pressure to line up my modest wardrobe with the designer wardrobes of the kids around me. I recall wishing we had the money to afford a new pair of Levi's jeans but settling for one of those discounted outlets where you can buy a "slightly defective" product. Maybe you've noticed the orange tag on the back of a pair of Levi's. In order to clarify the reject status of the jeans, the outlets tore off the orange tag. Not to be out-smarted, I found a pair of old (legitimate) Levi's, cut out the precious orange tag, then proceeded to sew it onto the cheaper pair I had bought.

It's an embarrassing memory, but we could fill this book with a host of other, darker stories of the ways we humans try to patch together some sort of "righteousness" to get us on the "inside" of some location we can't put our finger on.

"You are different." That comment can be taken two very different ways. When we are kids in the schoolyard, it is the phrase we most fear. At some base level, we need to fit in, and any difference, any oddity, has to be tucked in or tapered off if we expect to survive socially. To be seen as different is to be seen with disdain. Later in life, when people are tired of fitting in, when everyone has at some point wrestled with their own existential loneliness, those same words can be the height of flattery.

Here is the difficulty: we are hard-wired to become someone significant and make a difference. The fact is, we can't shake this internal craving to matter. It's part of being crafted in the image of God.

When we want to fit in with the masses, we have an implicit trust in the system or social structure we opt into. Years later when we want to be different it is because we have lost faith in that system or those people or at least grown bored with it.

ALIENS IN THE WORLD WE LIVE IN

On one hand we recognize that "God so loves the world." When it comes to the people, the tribes, the humanity that populate planet earth, God has great affection. He adores humanity with a love beyond words. But there is another side of "the world" to which Scripture speaks more severely.

> Do not love the world or the things in the world. If anyone loves the world, the love of the Father is not in him. For all that is in the world – the lust of the flesh and the lust of the eyes and pride of life – is not from the Father but from the world.[4]

Holiness always manifests within the context of the world we live in. This is the holiness challenge. Somehow we need to follow our God by loving the world—but not loving the world. We love the *people* of the world, but we oppose the *systems* of the world.

The challenge is complex because every Christian, leader, and church is confronted with a different version of "the world." You can count on some version of pride and lust, but how it manifests itself will vary. It's different at every age. It varies from continent to continent. And yet the sway is ever-present and often subtle. Like a slow-moving river, one barely detects its current— and rarely fights it—unless it is recognized. If you are not aware of it, you will not counteract it, and herein lies the problem. The world as we know it needs a redemptive alien touch that can only be brought by people who act like the aliens they really are. You never change the world by being like the world. Aliens have to embrace their identity. Difference makers must be different. It takes holiness. Contextualized holiness.

I remember talking to a Cuban pastor about his observations regarding Christianity in the context of American culture. "I feel so sorry for you," he told me. That was stunning to come from a man who has spent seasons of his life imprisoned for his faith. When I asked why he felt sorry for us he responded, "Because it's so much harder to be a Christian here than in my country.

You have so many distractions to appeal to. So many lusts and so much pride." That would be *the world*. And the Bible says, "Come out."

The very term *church* refers to those who have been called out. The church is supposed to be a gathering of holy aliens who have embraced their peculiar identity, *fighting the sway of the world*, which is opposed to our Father, *for the sake of the world*, which is loved by our Father.

The base danger is to acquiesce, to give in to the seduction of the world. Worldliness always smells good. To sew the tag on the Levi's and try to fit in as comfortably as possible seems like such a reasonable approach. Churches do it all the time, yet the consistent feedback we get from seekers is that they don't explore Christianity for more of the same. They get it; they crave different.

Giving into the sway of the world is like falling off the left side of the gospel horse, but we humans have a dangerous proclivity. It seems that once we recognize the error of the left side we get back up, only to over-correct and fall off the right side. If we're not *seduced* by culture, we are prone to become *repulsed* by culture. In response to the overtly twisted nature of the world, many a believer has adopted the mantra: we are *in* the world, but we are not *of* the world. But their interpretation of this mantra often falls short. It's still anti-kingdom of God, because while Jesus was *in* the world and not *of* the world, he was still *for* the world.

Progressives and traditionalists are actually two sides of the same problem. The lawless and the legalist are two versions of the same worldly coin. They still play to our lusts and our pride. This is why our enemy has no problem with us leaving a life of alcohol-driven lust of the flesh, as long as we pick up a pride-driven religious smugness. This is why it's entirely possible to become an activist and give all your possessions to the poor, and still fall short in love as you give into a new set of worldly shackles. The way of holiness is neither progressive nor regressive; it is another option altogether. It's different. It's better.

IN CONTEXT

This plays itself out in a million ways. My children often ask if we could buy something that everybody else buys. Or if we can go to some place that others might go. Quite often the answer is no. *Is it because you don't make enough money?* No, it's this: we belong to the city of God, not the city of man. We're from the kingdom of heaven, not the world. That means we do things differently. We give God the firstfruit of every dollar we make. We remember the poor and the lost world because we are trying to be generous like our King. So yes, if we were of the world we could afford to do a lot of things we can't afford to do. In a culture of greed and opulence where charity is relegated to the end-of-the-month leftovers, we hear the call to be different. So we give. In a culture driven by fear of the unknown, we hear the invitation to step out and trust our invisible Provider.

We lead faith families that have chosen to give half of our resources to missions. We are fully aware that most churches give away about 3 percent of their income. Most Christians follow suit and give away about 3 percent of their income. That leaves about 3 percent of 3 percent of Christian wealth to ever touch the least and the lost of this world. Our 50 percent vision is an attempt to heed the call of a radically generous God and be different.

If you've ever tried to do an extended fast, you're going to feel the sway of the world as your body, church, and friends resist. Whatever else fasting may be, it is waiting. It is sacrifice. And the world I live in is about immediate gratification, immediate results, immediate feedback. One of the challenging realities to fasting is how little of anything you immediately receive in return for your efforts. And yet when you look in the rearview mirror, it's uncanny how much mileage you got from a season of afflicting your stomach. Few disciplines work holiness into a soul like fasting. In a culture of *now*, we hear the call to slow down and sacrifice.

What if seekers consider our faith, not because it's so similar to the natural lives they live, but because it has the possibility of actually being different? Supernaturally different. I wonder if we don't see more supernatural city of God activity because we're trying so hard to fit into the respectable nature of the city of man. Malcolm Muggeridge said that one of the most attractive things about Christianity is its sheer absurdity. We're aliens. Somehow we have to realize how thirsty our world is for *different*.

I love how the book of Acts describes the outcomes of the early church's awe-inspiring difference. Their lifestyle was so naturally supernatural that "none of the rest dared to join them..."[5] There are things we cannot do. We've been given new taste buds. And there are things we must do, regardless of how absurd they seem. Tell the truth no matter what the cost. Fulfill your marriage vows. Forgive your enemies. Turn the other cheek. Give to anybody who asks of you. Bless those who persecute you. Be a voice for the voiceless.

No one dared to join them. And yet, "Believers were increasingly added to the Lord, multitudes of both men and women."[6] What a sobering reality for a Christian who might be tempted to dumb down the message and dilute the discipleship call. The people of the city of man want the city of God, and they don't even know it. They have a soul-craving they can't put their finger on: it's called holiness. It will cost you to embrace it, but the only way to reach the world is to be an alien here, against the world, because we love the world.

The Apostle Peter had a peculiar take on sharing your faith: Live in a way that is so distinct, so odd, so *different*, that when people look at you they will ask you for a reason for the hope inside of you.[7] When was the last time somebody asked you for a reason for the hope you live in?

I love to hear the story of how people came to Jesus. I'll never forget a trip on a bus in another country where I met an absolutely precious woman. When I discovered she was a believer, I asked her to share her testimony. Here is the short version. "I was a teenager, and there was this one girl... she was just so different. I finally went to her and asked her what was so different about her. She responded by saying that she was the property of Jesus. When I left her I could not get the conversation out of my mind. So I went home and prayed this prayer: 'Jesus I want to be your property, too.'" Her life has never been the same.

You never change the world by being like the world; you change the world by embracing your identity. And you've been called out. You are an alien. So live like it.

What might this mean? First, stop trying to avoid the pain associated with the city of God. Stop being surprised when the world treats you like an alien. You feel like people are speaking evil about you at work? That is likely. You feel like your boss might overlook you for a promotion because of your faith? That's right. You feel like people talk about you behind your back? They will. It seems like your professors are tolerant of every belief but yours? True. If they did it to your King, they will do it to you. Your King was an alien. You are an alien. Stop being surprised when you're treated like one. Be holy.

Sometimes the protest will come from your own fallen flesh. The world has always been changed by those who embrace the way of Jesus, and there is no way of Jesus without sacrifice. But I'll promise you this: you won't be sorry.

Second, identify what you are to be set apart *from*. What part of the world has a particular sway on you? Get honest about this. It's always easier to identify the worldliness in any culture other than your own, or any other person other than you. Be humble enough to listen to the voice of your Father to identify the areas where you have loved the world. Is it the approval of man? Is it the desire for pleasure? Is it the inability to slow down and move to the rhythm of God's grace? When you see it, come out. This is called repentance.

Then, get clear about what you have been set apart for. Embrace the call to be both against the world and for the world. The heritage of the Hebrews 11 heroes was not a detached life of world-avoidance, but a fully immersed life of blessing the world. Salt with flavor. Light turned on. The heroes of our faith are those people who set their minds on the heavenly city in such a way that they can't help but pray and become the answer to the Lord's prayer: Your kingdom come, Your will be done on earth as it is in heaven. We fully engage; we address darkness wherever we find it; we bless the very world that persecutes us.

You never change the world by being like the world. God's people have always been peculiar, separate, and distinct. And this is our burden. Too many Christians have settled for more of the same. Salt that loses its flavor. Light that does not shine. Indistinct. It's *unholy*. Why are we so tempted to try to spin our city of God to be accepted by a city of man that will never have the eyes to get it? Let's go be who we are. Be holy.

Enoch had a challenge unlike that of Moses. Abraham's challenge was not the same as Augustine's. Martin Luther's challenge was not likely yours. And yet God's people have always been called out. This is not a minor theme in Scripture. Like a constant refrain, the church is called out:

> Therefore go out from their midst, and be separate from them, says the Lord, and touch no unclean thing; then I will welcome you, and I will be a Father to you, and you will be sons and daughters to me, says the Lord Almighty.[8]

If you fully grasped this invitation you'd have goose bumps right now. What was done in the Garden has been undone by the Cross. Jesus has made a way. We are truly welcome. We really do belong. Just not here. To the extent that we line up our practical life of action with our positional life of righteousness, we will experience the welcome of God. Intimacy with the Father we long to know. Citizenship on the inside of a place we know we were made for, a place of intimacy, purpose, praise and marvelous light.

> But you are a chosen generation, a royal priesthood, a holy nation, a peculiar people; that you should show forth the praises of him who has called you out of darkness into his marvelous light.[9]

If you want to know more about what that could look like, read on.

ONE

TWO

THREE

FOUR

FIVE

SIX

SEVEN

EIGHT

NINE

TEN

ELEVEN

TWELVE

Jesus and the Fullness of Time

"Happy families are all alike; every unhappy family is unhappy in its own way."[1] What makes us holy (different) is also what makes us the same, a joy in the centrality and sufficiency of Jesus. Jesus makes us different by uniting us in a common love for him. The people of God must be the people of Jesus. We can have no other gods before him, including lesser versions of Jesus. We must be infatuated, inspired, and involved with him because all theology is Christology (who we say he is). It is not just the Jesus of the past that we seek and worship, but the present and future Jesus presented in Scripture that is our savior and king.

In his important and eye opening book, *Bad Religion: How We Became a Nation of Heretics,* New York Times columnist Ross Douthat evaluates the last 100 years of American Christianity in a sweeping history full of insight and honesty. He chronicles the rise and fall of American mainline churches and comes to the conclusion that Christianity is not so much in decline as it is changing. The real threat to orthodox Christianity, he argues, is not unbelief but false belief, not people losing interest in God but allowing heretics to define him. Heretical theologies have become mainstream. The church is alive and well. It is just not looking like the church of history.

JESUS, THE WHOLE JESUS, SO HELP ME GOD

It is increasingly en vogue to strip Jesus of his more difficult characteristics, leaving those who worship this new Jesus with what Douthat calls a "conviction deficit." The newly revealed Jesus didn't believe in hell, didn't warn the world about the evil of wealth, denied suffering, made the kingdom easy to understand and easy to enter. If we would believe it, Jesus was a self-actualizing, money-making, pain-avoidance system. In short, Jesus was just like us. We have taken a Jesus who is by nature different from us and who calls us to be different from the person we currently are and reshaped him in our own image.

Aside from being wrong, this kind of revisionist Christology has not only obscured the most important figure in our lives, it has damaged the listener. A false Christ cannot save. The irony here is that the Jesus that has been stripped of his prophetic voice is a Jesus who is impotent to do anything for us. This revised Jesus cannot improve you, or offer you your best life, or make you healthy, wealthy, or wise. If Jesus cannot judge us, then he is not able to rescue us either. This mythical Jesus is meant to be a friendlier and more life-affirming character but is just as unreal as a unicorn. We only really have one enduring choice when it comes to Jesus; accept him as he is. His person is static and unchanging. He is the one who was, is, and is to come.

It is precisely the paradox of his personality that holds the mystery of his revelation. If we try to domesticate him we only hurt ourselves. Douthat agrees that the paradox of Jesus' character is what makes him unique, and we tamper with it at our own peril:

> No figure in history or fiction contains as many multitudes as the New Testament's Jesus. He's a celibate ascetic who enjoys dining with publicans and changing water into wine at weddings. He's an apocalyptic prophet one moment, a wise ethicist the next. He's a fierce critic of Jewish religious law who insists that he's actually fulfilling rather than subverting it. He preaches a reversal of every social hierarchy while deliberately avoiding explicitly political claims. He promises to set parents against children and then disallows divorce; he consorts with prostitutes while denouncing lustful thoughts. He makes wild claims about his own relationship to God, and perhaps his own divinity, without displaying any of the usual signs of megalomania or madness. He can be egalitarian and hierarchical, gentle and impatient, extraordinarily charitable and extraordinarily

judgmental. He sets impossible standards and then forgives the worst sinners. He blesses the peacemakers and then promises that he's brought not peace but a sword. He's superhuman one moment; the next he's weeping. And of course the accounts of his resurrection only heighten these paradoxes by introducing a post crucifixion Jesus who is somehow neither a resuscitated body nor a flitting ghost but something even stranger still—a being at once fleshly and supernatural, recognizable and trans-figured, bearing the wounds of the crucifixion even as he passes easily through walls. The boast of Christian orthodoxy... has always been its fidelity to the *whole of Jesus*.[2]

By contrast, he concludes the goal of all great heresies is to extract from the tension of Jesus's story the paradoxes, leaving him neat and easily comprehendible. But as the late Scottish divine James Stewart explained, "There is nothing in history like the union of contrast which confronts us in the gospels. *The mystery of Jesus is the mystery of divine personality.*"[3]

It is the parts we find hardest to understand that make him Lord. The first and possibly only real call to be different in this world is a call to be like Jesus, to understand and obey him as Lord. That means there will be pieces of his life and teaching which are self-evident and easy to obey and other pieces that require faith. That will require us to believe that he knows, that he is still the teacher, and that we are still the students. When we pick and choose the teaching and characteristics of Jesus we want to obey, we recreate him in our own image and destroy the one who can actually save us. It is in the places we find it hard to submit to him that our redemption is confined. And his own words echo in the caverns of disobedient lives, "You call me 'Teacher' and 'Lord,' and rightly so, for that is what I am... you should do as I have done."[4]

OUR JUDGE *AND* OUR REDEEMER

I (Brian) recently spoke at the major university in my city. A student group built a giant canvas in the middle of campus, inviting students to write down their questions about God. It was an affirmation of the place of inquiry in the life of the heart and mind. They invited me in for the final event, to try to address the bigger meta questions and to offer a theology that could answer them.

After the event, one student waited behind to ask me a question. Musing on the idea that Jesus is/was punished for our crimes, and in his death that justice is somehow satisfied, he asked, "How would it be moral for God to punish someone who is innocent for my crimes?" In other words, if I have done wrong, how is it justice to punish another person for that wrong and then to let me go free? I was really impressed with the question and the genuine heart I sensed behind it. You see, most students who reject the gospel do so because they do not think they deserve any punishment. A smaller percentage might agree they do and then are happy to accept that someone would take the fall for them, not considering the implications to the one who takes the fall. This young man was pressing into a critical Christological necessity.

"Because," I told him, "the one who judges is also the one who was wronged. The one who was wronged is also the one who takes the fall for you."

It would be immoral for the judge to place our punishment on another, but for the judge to place the punishment on himself? This is the breathtaking height of moral perfection. Jesus is the one who is sinned against. All sin is a sin against God. And God judges that sin, and then lays his just judgment on his own head.

Jesus reveals that God loves us as he judges us. He reveals an ingenious, magnanimous God who is not essentially angry or distant or irascible. And this is just the beginning of what we learn about God by looking into the face of Jesus:

> For God, who said, 'Let light shine out of darkness,' made his
> light shine in our hearts to give us the light of the knowledge
> of God's glory displayed in the face of Christ.[5]

Christology is a bridge between the transcendent God who created the universe and the limited senses of human knowledge. How do we see the God who cannot be seen? How do we understand the God who speaks and worlds are created? Paul, John, and the rest of the New Testament writers give us the answer. We can look into the face of Christ. The depths of God are suddenly accessible because we can look at him.

WIDE EYED THEOLOGY

If the goal of Scripture is the revelation of God (theology) then that revelation finds its highest point, its more luminous moment, in the flash of lightning that is the life of Jesus (Christology). All theology (and all of the Bible) culminates in and radiates from the coming (and the telling of that coming) of Jesus.

The Messianic age is the brokering of a New Covenant between God and his people, and that covenant comes to us in what Augustine first called the *totus Christus,* the complete life of Jesus.[6] Not just his incarnation, or his revolutionary teaching, or his miracles of healing and deliverance, or even just the cross without the resurrection. Each of these is an invaluable part of the whole. But the attempt to reduce the gospel, Christology, or theology to just one of these is a problem, because it is all of these things taken together that offers a complete, comprehensive revelation, perfect in its construction and prophetic in its purpose. When others want to dismantle, minimize or otherwise distort Jesus we must be different in holding to all that he is, does, and teaches. A ruthless Christology is the heart of honest discipleship and true worship because Christology is the beginning and end of all theology.

To say as Paul said to the church at Corinth, "For I resolved to know nothing while I was with you except Jesus Christ and him crucified" is to make a resolution of extraordinary proportions. It is to resolve to know all that there is to know about God. It is a Christocentric statement but not a statement reducing the life, teaching, death, resurrection, and promised return to the moment of crucifixion alone. In the line preceding this one he calls his message "the testimony about God." It is a reminder of the *totus Christus* and an assertion that all theology finds its way to Jesus.

He is a vision of the invisible God. What was unseen, unknown, and impossibly hidden before has now been revealed. In Jesus. Consider the words of prologue to Hebrews (for Jews) and Colossians (for Gentiles):

> In the past God spoke to our ancestors through the prophets at many times and in various ways, but in these last days he has spoken to us by his Son, whom he appointed heir of all things, and through whom also he made the universe. The Son is the radiance of God's glory and the exact representation of his being, sustaining all things by his powerful word.[7]

> The Son is the image of the invisible God, the firstborn over all creation. For in him all things were created: things in heaven and on earth, visible and invisible, whether thrones or powers or rulers or authorities; all things have been created through him and for him. He is before all things, and in him all things hold together. And he is the head of the body, the church; he is the beginning and the firstborn from among the dead, so that in everything he might have the supremacy. For God was pleased to have all his fullness dwell in him, and through him to reconcile to himself all things, whether things on earth or things in heaven, by making peace through his blood, shed on the cross.[8]

If expressed chronologically, the Old Testament builds toward the Messianic age, and the Gospels, Acts and the Epistles are about life in the Messianic age, and finally the Revelation is about the age to come. Irenaeus called the word of Jesus and the spirit of Jesus the two hands of God. [9]

THE FULLNESS OF GOD AND THE FULLNESS OF TIME
On the first day of his public ministry, Jesus, having returned from his trial in the desert, sits in the place of visiting Rabbi in

his hometown synagogue. He is handed the scroll of the prophet Isaiah, and he took it and opened it to Isaiah 61. So much of Isaiah is pregnant with Messianic expectation; the chapter he chooses to read from, more than any other, captured the Messianic hope of impoverished Nazareth. "The spirit of the Lord is upon me because he has anointed me to bring good news to the poor."[10] Jesus is establishing both his messianic identity and the entrance of the listening generation into a new age. He is saying, "This is the year of the Lord's favor, and I am the one on whom the Spirit of the sovereign Lord rests."

Aside from the description of his messianic ministry, and the implications of God's favor in the world being good news for the poor, the blind, and the imprisoned, it is just as significant what he does not read, because he stops the text in mid-sentence.

He leaves off the second half of Isaiah's thought. "...the year of the Lords favor and the day of vengeance of our God."[11] His omission does not invalidate the vengeance. It simply postpones it.

For his audience the consensus was that the day of the Messiah was a day of grace AND judgement. Sometimes called the "great and terrible day of the Lord" there was an expectation of undivided reckoning; that the righteous would be vindicated and the evil punished in one massive Messianic gesture. It would be great for those he comes to save—the poor and the abused—and it would be terrible for those who he came to judge—the abusers. Yet Jesus seems to want to separate this day into two days. This means that Christology then, must be seen as two movements in the great story of God. In his first coming he brings healing, salvation, hope, grace, and the almost unbelievable promise of reconciliation with God. He brings the promise of a stay of execution of the justice of God against the enemies of God. In turn, in the second coming he will bring with him the justice that has long been denied the oppressed and finally make right all that is wrong in the world. He will come at first to offer the world a second chance and then finally to reckon with the choice each of us has made.

This means that Christology is not just a look at the first century Rabbi Jesus of Nazareth, but it is an attempt to understand God, the whole character and person of God.

The weight and importance of this task cannot be understated. It is, simply put, the most important thing a person can do. Who do you say that I am? The question that lies at the heart of the gospels is also the question for the life of every spiritual seeker and the bull's eye of the work of disciples and theologians alike. The resounding answer from the whole New Testament, codified in the first and earliest creed of the church is, "Jesus is Lord."

The embodied declaration of that creed is a distinguishing feature of the church and the people of God. Holiness is impossible without its honest proclamation. We have to remember that creed, and define ourselves by not just saying it but living as if it were true. To come to the conclusion that he is not only Lord of heaven and earth, but he is Lord over me. To live as if he were not just the master of life and death, but that he is the master of my life, and when the time comes, my death. That he is not just the author of all life, but that he is the one writing my story. That he is not only the Lord of history and King in the future, but that he is Lord of my past, present, and future.

Paul asserted that "no one can say, 'Jesus is Lord,' except by the Spirit of God,"[12] because to say and live by those words is to surrender the fullness of our lives, the locus of its control, to Jesus. Maybe this is the simplest definition of a disciple: someone who has made Jesus everything. Followers who have not made Jesus the first of many priorities but who have made Jesus our only priority; the one that governs the rest.

This is not something that is done easily, but when it is done it recreates the person into the image of the one they follow. Imitation becomes worship and worship becomes holiness. And holiness will awaken a slumbering world. He does not just reveal the truth about God to us but the truth about ourselves, and who we were meant to be. He shows us how to be human and to live as a child of God and a servant to his purposes. Watching Jesus teaches us everything we need to know about life and God.

THE JESUS WHO WAS

But the challenge is to try and hold tight to a Jesus that cannot be completely defined, to seek him alone, and to let him continue to grow larger in the perception of our hearts and minds. In part, that means stubbornly holding on to what we have learned while continuing, like a child, to search for what we have yet to see and understand. In that way, Jesus is like the natural world he has created; you can love it because of what you have come to know, but still long for vistas of beauty yet uncovered.

This means that we want to become people who refuse to dehumanize, trivialize, or minimize Jesus. We want to be people who embrace the whole life of Jesus and who hold on to the mystery of his paradoxes.

We want to be people who listen to the words of Jesus and let them cut us, remembering that he is Lord and that we are the ones who have to change in hearing them, not him who has to change to fit our lifestyles or life choices.

We want to be people who remember that Jesus was a little wild, like his cousin from the desert. That he was a prophet without fear of religion, institution, government, or pop culture.

We want to remember that Jesus was a lover and warrior for the poor, who himself lived the life of a wanderer and a beggar. That he was a man who befriended, inspired, loved, and empowered the castoffs of society.

We want to remember that Jesus who spoke a hard word to the rich, but who made room for them, too. To remember the Jesus who came first to love and comes soon to judge.

We want to remember that Jesus who lived and worked as a part of a small, intentional community. If ever there was a man who did not need community, it was Jesus. He was totally sufficient in himself, yet he showed us that life is best lived in the company of others.

This is the same Jesus who would shake up the world with the unthinkable notions of equality and human dignity. A man who went out of his way to befriend and honor women and children, the diseased and the outcast, the worst sinners and every ethnic group he met. The same Jesus who bent the laws of nature at a whim and who said greater things than these will you do in my name. The same Jesus who called and who continues to call ordinary people to be different, and in holiness, to change the world in his name.

But we are not just calling for the Jesus of history to be fully represented, it is not just the Jesus of the Gospels that has been misrepresented; it is the Jesus that stands outside of time. It is God himself who is misunderstood because of our weak Christology.

THE JESUS WHO IS AND EVER SHALL BE

You see, we cannot just think about Jesus in the past tense because he is not dead. We have to be different in seeing not just all of who he was, but who he currently is and who he has promised he will be.

This kind of Christology will produce a new kind of disciple, making up revolutionary churches. In his prologue to his revelation, John describes the Jesus he encounters as "Him who is, who was, and who is to come... the firstborn from among the dead."[13]

We tend to think of people in history a certain way. We refer to them in the past tense because that is where they lived and where they belong in any sane retelling of the events that included them. We hold them there, as we should, in the past, in the time and space where they lived. Jesus in that sense is not a historical figure.

John is saying that Jesus was, yes, a person in history. But he is saying he is also a contemporary and futuristic figure as well. We simply have no corresponding category that can help us to comprehend him except of course for our notion of God. The first thing John does in his expansive Christology is establish Jesus as

Lord over not just us, his churches and the kings of the earth, but over time itself. He is from the past, he is here now in our present, and he is coming to reign over the future.

The Jesus we know from the gospels; the Nazarene, who comes as a child, who fasts in the desert, who heals, whose identity was a secret, who lived among the poor, who had virtually no earthly power showed us how to be strong when we are weak and how to be great when we are small. His story ends when he lets us kill him to show us the meaning and strength of real love.

That Jesus was mocked and said nothing. That Jesus fulfilled the promise of Isaiah that "like a sheep before its shearers he did not say a word."[14] He was beaten, tortured, falsely accused, and he endured it all for love.

But that same Jesus did not just die, he also rose. He was dead, but he came back from that death different. And like a caterpillar changes in its chrysalis, he changed in the tomb. The Lamb of God, the Prince of Peace, became violent. He took death and the devil by the throat, and he demanded his life back. And not just his own life. But mine and yours, too.

He said, "Give me Brian's life. Give me Mike's life.

I am the maker of heaven and earth.

I am the first and the last.

I am the one who was and is and is to come.

I am the Lord of heaven and earth.

I am life itself, and the Lord of both space and time.

Give me that life back."

And hell screamed as its grip was broken, and as it gave up the dead. And he rescued those whom he had chosen since before the foundations of the world were laid.

And the angels sang, and the earth shook from the sheer force of it. But what no human being saw that day was the world splitting open and the grave giving up its contraband, as the author of life burst forth with a book of names in his hands.

And the gospel record says that he appeared to his followers. But he was different. He was glorified, and so they worshiped him.

And he let them until his ascension to the Father's side. All of that is just describing the Jesus who was. We are right to worship him. But to see Jesus for who he really is we must also learn to know and love and worship the Jesus who is now (the glorified savior) and the Jesus who will be (the conquering king).

THE HEIGHTS OF WORSHIP

A full Christology should take the breath away and keep the heart full. It will fill our heads with wonder and give our hands work to do. It is this kind of wide-eyed theology that will keep our heads in the clouds and our feet on the ground, making us a different kind of church for a watching world.

My (Brian) youngest daughter, Eve, has a Quaker Parrot. She calls him Charlie. He's a beautiful green bird that talks, loves no one so much as Eve, and who unfortunately cannot fly. This bird had its wings clipped; a procedure that I understand is common and possibly even necessary in order to keep a bird like Charlie. But there are few things sadder than watching a bird with clipped wings try to fly.

On the rare occasion that Charlie gets out of his cage, he always tries to fly away. I find this odd. Since he was a baby he has not been able to successfully fly. Charlie has never known any reality other than a flightless one. Yet still he stubbornly, perhaps instinctively, tries to fly. In his experience, birds are lousy at flying, and you would think he would give up on it. I find him to be a sad but resilient reflection of modern Christianity.

God made us to fly. Somewhere deep inside us, when we reflect on God, read his word, find him in the secret place of prayer, we know it. But somehow our wings have been cut. We listen to lifeless sermons, watch unimpressive lives, and we have never really experienced what it is like to soar on the wind, light but powerful. But still we try to know him, to seek him, as we squint at the inadequate portraits of Jesus we see painted. We were made to worship. But we have never felt the virtue of a full wingspan, of a whole Christology, we have never known anything but the cage of our cultural Jesus, locked in time.

To see him for all that he is releases us to worship him in a way we instinctively know we should. To behold the fullness of Jesus is to fly. And to fly with him is to experience the greatest wholeness and life a person can know. Christians that are awestruck by the mystery and wonder of Jesus are tangibly holy, different in the way that matters most.

ONE
TWO

THREE

FOUR
FIVE
SIX
SEVEN
EIGHT
NINE
TEN
ELEVEN
TWELVE

Fairy Tales and the Non-Conformity of Grace

It is by gazing on Jesus that we find the most unexpected and liberating truth; he really knows and loves us. This revelation then becomes the foundation of our own identity, freeing us from the shame and power of sin in our lives. When our roots go deep into the love of God for us we become a new kind of person, recreated by that love and freed to love and bless the world that suffers without it.

For a number of years we had a bright, committed young woman, a part of our community, who wore a cape. Yes, a cape. Not like a super hero cape, more like an elf cape, or something medieval. It was emerald green and had a nice shimmer to it. At first blush, the cape would put you off, as you would wonder (even if you wouldn't say it) what is wrong with her? Like all non-conformity it challenged the status quo, drawing ire or admiration but rarely indifference. But as time went on, I came to really admire this daughter. We might wrongfully conclude that she lacked a certain social intelligence, but what if she was loved so deeply that she didn't care what we thought? I wondered if I could wear a cape, if I had the strength and security to follow her lead. Maybe she was out of touch or maybe she was just so loved that she was free.

BEING LOVED IS DIFFERENT

Her non-conformity became a kind of symbol for me. We ought to all be so loved. Are we too worried about what the world around us thinks or what they will say about us and our behavior that we don't walk in the fullness of our redemptive identity? Jesus has loved you so severely, so significantly, that he would see you truly freed to love, serve, and live for him. Consider the urging and logic of Paul in Romans 12:

> Therefore, I urge you, brothers and sisters, in view of God's mercy, to offer your bodies as a living sacrifice, holy and pleasing to God—this is your true and proper worship. Do not conform to the pattern of this world, but be transformed by the renewing of your mind.[1]

Non-conformity calls into question the validity of a system, culture, or practice. Without words it asks the provocative question, why? Why do we have to do it that way? The spirit of prophecy is the spirit that calls this world's order into question. Let's reason backwards with Paul and explore the connection between being loved, devotion to Jesus, and non-conformity.

We do not conform to this world because we have offered ourselves, all of our lives, to God. We have made that offering of our lives because we see how merciful he has been to us. It all begins with being loved. Love is the catalyst for worship in the same way that worship is the catalyst for non-conformity. People who are rooted in the love of God for them can live with surrender and abandon; they can refuse to conform to the world around them, offering that same world the redemption that they have tasted.

Perhaps we conform because we are not fully surrendered. And perhaps we are not fully surrendered because we have not grasped "how wide and long and high and deep is the love of Christ."[2]

It may seem like an elementary theme, but we are convinced that the people who root their hearts and lives in the immeasurable love of God and who gaze into the face of the one who loves them completely and totally are different. Then holiness is a feature of being loved, and God's love for us, while an objective reality, is rarely fully integrated in our view of ourselves and others. In other words, he loves us with a liberating love, but we need to constantly realize it for it to make a difference in our lives. So how can we do that?

CUTTING TIES WITH SHAME

Guilt is real. It comes from knowing what is right and then not doing it. We feel guilty for one of two reasons (or sometimes both). First, we feel guilty because we did wrong, and we are guilty. In that sense, we should not work so hard to get rid of our guilt, but to face it and ask for mercy. You cannot say you're sorry (really) unless you know you are wrong. Guilt in that way is like fear; on its face it is good because it helps us address reality with sobriety and honesty.

The second reason we feel guilt is because we are uncomfortable with forgiveness. We hold onto to our guilt in an attempt to punish ourselves. In this case guilt is unhealthy, because we do not understand the grace of God for us. When we are guilty, but have accepted the solution of Jesus, we can and should be free from that guilt. He alone can make our wrongs right, accounting for our sin and reconciling us to God. Still, sometimes we hold on to our guilt, refusing to believe or lay hold of the grace of God. This stubborn refusal is a new kind of rebellion blocking the gift of God and denying all reality, sobriety, and honesty. Your sin is bad and can produce guilt, but God is greater than your sin and your guilt!

Many of us still struggle with guilt in this way, but culturally guilt has become unfashionable and less prominent in our psychological landscapes. Shame, on the other hand, seems to be on the rise.

While guilt is a vertical phenomenon, alerting us to a breach of that first and most significant relationship, shame is more horizontal, alerting us to a breach in the social code. There are occasions when they overlap, but often they are actually opposed to each other. When we lie, we feel guilt, but we often feel shame if we tell the truth when a lie would have been the socially accepted norm. The truth teller is shamed more often than the liar. When we cheat on a test we feel guilt; we feel shame when we are honest, but fail that same test. If guilt is rooted in some awareness of absolute morality, then shame is rooted in the relative ambiguity of social expectation.

Social media is changing our reality because we are connected more loosely to more people than ever before. Our reality is very much determined by how we experience ourselves through the eyes of others; how others see us and feel about us. Our psyches have become Facebook walls where we see how popular we are and what people think about us and our ideas. Even deeper, we lose our sense of healthy guilt or awareness of objective morality because our center of moral gravity has shifted from a moral absolute (found in God) to popular opinion. We have traded a relationship with a good God for a variation of Social Proof Theory.[3] This is the demonstrated propensity that people without God have to attribute correctness to whatever the majority is doing. What is socially acceptable is proof of its acceptability. Without a vertical relationship with God we only understand right and wrong, good and evil, in terms of what everyone is else is doing.

This has made us more aware of the world than we are of any inner reality or awareness of God. We are therefore afraid of the world, choosing to work more on our image and the public's opinion of us rather than standing outside of the world's persuasions and loving it with power. The shift to shame has diminished the fear of God in us and increased the fear of the world.

The unbelieving world, while the object of our love and concern, is also the same group of people that Jesus said would hate us because they hated him.[4] It is the epitome of insanity to live our lives in search of the approval of a group of people that Jesus said would hate us. As in all things, Jesus is our example. He shows us how to love those around us, even our enemies, without living for their sanction.

There is an implication here that we will be hated in the same way that Jesus was hated. That we will stand out and against the culture where we live. That we will be different enough to draw the scorn of those who will not always understand us. Still, it is love that motivates us.

When we are loved deeply by God and when we allow that love to go down deep into the roots of our identity, we are able to be different, loving others completely while still remaining true to the heart of God in the midst of a depraved world. This requires an understanding of grace.

We are *justified* by grace through faith. And we are *sanctified* by grace through faith. Perhaps the greatest theological contribution of the Protestant Reformation was the second of these two statements. And perhaps the greatest theological challenge for most believers is precisely this: although they believe that the grace of God is sufficient to justify, forgive, and pardon them, they functionally believe that future growth and progress will be the result of their own self-effort. In other words, Jesus got this ball rolling, but I'll have to take it from here.

Here is the issue. When we allow our *sanctification* (ongoing progress) to feed on our *justification* (finished work), we thrive. But when the opposite occurs, we base the stability of our justification on the instability of our sanctification, and we fall deeper into the guilt cycle. It was the unmerited favor and work of Jesus that saved us, and it is the unmerited favor and work of Jesus that grows us. This is why Paul said that all he talked about was Christ and him crucified.[5] Apparently, every word of wisdom and moral exhortation was directly tied back to the gospel of grace.

This means the key to *growing* in the Kingdom is the same key to getting in the Kingdom: a life-altering encounter with the amazing grace of God. It is the good news (about what Jesus has done and is doing), not the good advice (about what *we do*) or the bad news (about what we have or have not done). While our teaching must include moral imperatives and instruction, it must find its roots in the finished work of the cross and the ongoing work of the Spirit. Gospel freedom, not legalistic shame, is the fuel for every call to obedience and mission.

Thus, transformation is not the result of trying harder, but beholding more deeply the grace and person of Jesus. Just as the serpent was lifted up in the wilderness, when the people gazed upon it, they were changed. When we gaze upon Christ and his finished work, we are transformed because we realize, we are His. The shame is gone. As we lead people to know who they are, they will increasingly act out of that new identity.

RECEIVING A NEW NAME

Paul begins his letter to the church in Corinth, arguably one of the most dysfunctional and worldly churches in the first century, with this greeting:

> To the church of God in Corinth, to those sanctified in Christ Jesus and called to be his holy people, together with all those everywhere who call on the name of our Lord Jesus Christ— their Lord and ours...[6]

On the one hand, he uses the past tense, referring to them as "those sanctified," and on the other hand he uses the future tense, defining them as those that are "called to be holy." This is the paradox of Christian identity. We are already holy (set apart) because of events God has already put into motion, and yet we are called to be holy (different) as we live in the light of those events. We are loved, but we have to remember that and live like we know it.

Names are powerful things. How we name things is equally powerful to the one that names and the one(s) named. How others see me effects what they call me and in turn effects how I see myself. How I see myself has a major influence on what I do and how I act, bringing it full circle to how others see me.

If I (Brian) believe myself to be an honest man, when I am given the opportunity to be honest, I am more likely to tell the truth. And if I think of myself as a faithful husband, then when faced with the temptation to be unfaithful I will find it dissonant and at odds with my own sense of self. I will not reject it so much because I am strong, but because of how I see myself, which is at odds with the behavior being offered. I won't do it because I will think, "That's just not me." The critical question then becomes, "Who gets to define you?"

For the 19th century sociologist, Charles Cooley, that person is whoever is most important to you.[7] If that entity is God, a parent, a friend, a lover, or all your twitter followers, you will tend to view yourself in the mirror of their definition of you. In other words, we tend to think we are whatever the most important person in our lives thinks we are.

To this day, I still believe I could have been good at ballet because my mother, who was a professional dancer, always said so. Whether that is objectively true or not is not at issue; it is what I believe, and it comes totally from her authoritative view of me.

If we say to one of our children, "You are a genius," and then they fail a test at school, will they be more likely to question their genius or will they question the validity of the test? We can both testify that our children (brimming with confidence from the unconditional love and confidence of their authoritative fathers) always question the test.

What has Paul heard about this young church in Corinth? That they have succumbed to sexual sin, division, excess in worship, disputes in the city, that they are critical of his leadership, and that they are forgetting the heart of the gospel. And yet, he does not name them that way. He reminds them of the name that God has called them, saints.

Social scientists call the effects of naming a self-fulfilling prophecy or the Pygmalion effect. When we think something negative or positive about a person, it tends to come true because we alter the context enough to make it come true, or we alter our perception enough to believe it is true.

What happens then when we know ourselves as beloved? This is the radical psychological impact of the gospel when a sinner grasps the infinite greatness, holiness, and power of God while simultaneously realizing that he knows us, names us, and is filled with affection toward us. Knowing that we are the beloved of God then causes us to live differently. John connects the stunning realization that we are loved by God as children with the purification process that leads to holiness. "See what great love the Father has lavished on us, that we should be called children of God! And that is what we are... All who have this hope in him purify themselves, just as he is pure."[8] If this reality eclipsed all others, wouldn't the result be a different kind of Christian and a different kind of church?

Jacob was renamed after a night of struggle with God. The man he wrestled asked Jacob the profound question, "What is your name?" His identity as a liar and a hustler is replaced by a new name, Israel. When Jesus wanted to shape the emerging leadership of a fisherman and friend named Simon, he started calling him Peter (rock). He would interchange those names in the gospel narrative, calling him Simon when he acted like the old man and Peter when we was living into the identity of his new name.

I have nicknames for all my children. Names that I have given them that no one else uses but me. Jella, Bubba, Pooter, Dukey, Squidward, and Chachie. Not particularly meaningful, but they are mine. I do not use their nicknames when they are in trouble, only when they are safely in the good graces of my affection. When I call them by these names, they know that all is well.

Renaming is a gift that God gives to all his children. I am moved by the image of Revelation 2:17 and the promise that the glorified Jesus gives to those who overcome. "I will also give that person a white stone with a new name written on it, known only to the one who receives it." The name he gives us is both intimate and permanent. It is known only to us, and yet it is etched in stone. It is forever but it is personal, like no other word that will ever be spoken to us.

BELIEVING THE TRUE FAIRY TALE

Not long ago my youngest son told a story about his older brother Simeon. The story began, "Simeon is a dinosaur." This is a good story precisely because Simeon is not a dinosaur. It is a good story because it calls on our imagination. It asks us to believe something about Simeon that is not yet true. I am convinced that we are not telling each other the right story.

All of us need to remember and retell the story of a God so in love with his wayward creation that he refused to abandon them. A God revealed in Jesus Christ that, while we were yet sinners, saw us as more and chose to love, lead, and die for us. "I am the beloved of God," is no less fantastic than, "Simeon is a dinosaur." Faith is more but it is also not less than an exercise in imagination. When Paul calls the Corinthian church saints, he sees what it is that God wants them to become, and what in a very real sense they already are because God has set his mind to make them that way. The new names that God gives us are only laid hold of by faith. We must dare to believe that our wildest dreams are true, that our sin is not our defining characteristic, but that his love for us is.

Both of us have taken the naming of our children very seriously. We have done a lot of naming, since we have 14 kids between us (True at printing. There may be more now; you never know with Mike and Ruth). When we name our children we always pray, asking God to reveal a name more than to give a name. It is our conviction that God already knows them, who they will become, and who he wants them to be. For that reason we give our children names that we hope, in some general way, will shape the course of their lives. In a very real sense, we expect their name will define them. Does the name influence who they become? Or does the name anticipate (see into the future) what they were always going to be? Maybe a bit of both; we don't know. The aggregate effect is the same. Jael is motivated to see justice done. Noah is faithful when no one else is. Eve is a lover of God through nature. Luke is a sensitive healer. Simeon is a profoundly deep thinker, solitary, yet close to God. But here is the living principle: As we have named them, so they are. Who has named you? Where do you look for your understanding of yourself? What story do you tell?

Paul writes his letter to address a series of problems, challenges, and questions facing the Corinthian church. Frankly, he had heard some scandalous things, things that have broken his heart. But his vision of them is theocentric. The story he tells is the story of God.

He does not deny their flaws and their error (he will spend the rest of the book dealing with them), but he sees the more profound reality guiding his hand and his answers. God has called you, and he is faithful. In another place he would muse, "Even when we are faithless, he remains faithful." And, "He who began a good work in you will see it to completion."[9] God makes covenant with himself, because there is no one else to swear by. Your unfaithfulness does not change him, and it will not foil his work in you. The best way I know to say it is this: what God starts, he finishes. God has made a promise to himself to finish the work he has started in you.

LETTING GRACE RECEIVED BECOME GRACE GIVEN

If we are right and as we argued in the last chapter, Christology is the center of all theology, then grace is at the center of Christology. The core revelation found in the life of Jesus is that God is motivated out of a deep and intractable love for us. Jesus reveals that God is our Father, and that while he is holy, his intentions for us are good, and he is willing to give all he has to give in order to restore our relationship with him. The cross, which is the fulcrum of Christology, demonstrates once and for all that we cannot save ourselves but that God's indomitable love can. We are adopted as sons and daughters, not because of something we have done or could ever do, but because we are the unexpected objects of God's marvelous affections. This is called grace, or undeserved preference.

Still, our ongoing condition as stubborn sinners leaves us disconnected from the implications of grace. It is like we have been given an indescribable gift, but we have yet to open it. Like we have been set free from a life sentence in prison, but we still won't leave, or if we do, we come back at night to sleep in our cell. This liberation is not just for us; it is for all those we can now love because we are free.

Letting the experience of God's gracious love be the defining reality of our lives does not just change our self-image (who we think we are), it also changes our posture toward others (who we think they are). Jesus very plainly taught that people who are unmerciful have not believed themselves to be the recipients of great mercy.[10] The more we understand the breadth of the love and forgiveness of God, the more forgiving we are to those who wrong us.

Off and on throughout the first three centuries of the church, Christians suffered under Roman persecution. There were periods of intense suffering, torture, and even death that came to be commonplace in the life of the church. Named Christians would be forced to make an offering, burning incense to the Roman God-man and declaring that, "Caesar is Lord." This was of course the one thing a Christian could not do and many held to their witness that only Jesus was Lord, holding up to torture, and often death for defying their civic duty to worship Caesar. Those who died were of course revered as martyrs and symbols of fidelity. Those who were tortured, but who survived without conceding, were called the "confessors." A kind of living martyr, they were deeply respected by all Christians.

There was another group, however, who acquiesced under the threat. There were those who succumbed to the pressure, made the sacrifice, and said the blasphemous words. They were called the "lapsed." The problem that the church then faced was what to do with the lapsed.

Often repentant and ashamed of their betrayal, the lapsed would seek conciliation in the church. Should they be accepted back into the community? Wasn't the church supposed to be place of forgiveness and grace? And yet, how can we honor the memory and lives of martyrs and the confessors if we just let them back in? So, the church was divided over the issue.

One third century Bishop, Cyprian of Carthage, took the hard line that the lapsed should not be allowed fellowship in the church, refusing them absolution, and even moved for their excommunication. His position might have been somewhat tenable if it were not for the background of his own story. Cyprian himself, shortly after his conversion, was confronted by a wave of persecution in North Africa. Unlike Polycarp or other bishops who boldly presented themselves, and gladly accepted martyrdom as examples to their flocks of steadfast faith, Cyprian fled. When he was tested he had failed, yet he remained intolerant of the lapsed.

In a profoundly important twist of irony, the group that most disputed his hard line position against forgiving and including the lapsed were the confessors. Those who had themselves suffered for their faith believed the lapsed should be allowed penance, then forgiven and be fully restored into the fellowship of the church. The revelation here is that the more righteous a person is the more gracious they are. The more a person receives and understands grace the more freely they will give it. If you don't give grace easily to others, it could be because you have not understood it for yourself. Those who refuse grace do so because they are foreigners to it.

Maybe I reject a certain kind of sinner because I am afraid I am that person. So, I condemn them, creating a moral distance from that identity and the sin I fear in myself. Because if I offer them grace or minimize that sin I am somehow agreeing with it, and in turn communicating my sympathy for it in myself. All because we are not finding our identity (and therefore our freedom) as loved sinners.

Cyprian was ungracious because he had not really received grace himself. Paul is gracious because he had. He knew, deep down, that calling this church "saints" was no more ludicrous than calling himself an apostle. These are the names God gives to those on whom he has set his affections. His love is that powerful. Remembering that will make us different.

It is not just for ourselves that we have to understand and remember the love of God, it is also for others. The kingdom will not come through a people who have not allowed it to come into their hearts. The reign of darkness inside our own heads comes to an end when Jesus is allowed to rule. His first act as king of our lives is to declare us loved, known, and accepted by him. He gives us a new name to live into and calls us to sink deep roots into the soil of his view of us. We are sinners, but we are loved anyway. This otherworldly grace changes us, making us holy, and shows us a new way to live.

So, we "pray that the eyes of your heart may be enlightened in order that you may know the hope to which he has called you, the riches of his glorious inheritance in his holy people, and his incomparably great power for us who believe."[11]

ONE
TWO
THREE
FOUR
FIVE
SIX
SEVEN
EIGHT
NINE
TEN
ELEVEN
TWELVE

"COULD YOU NOT WATCH WITH
ME FOR ONE HOUR?"
MARK 14:37

Shut Doors and Intimacy with God

*It is possible to know a lot about God and very little of God.
We can change everything else about ourselves but if we do
not know God intimately we will offer no real solutions to the
needs and longing of our own hearts and certainly not those of
the world.*

Sometimes I (Mike) ask questions I should not ask. Especially
with married couples. The mild version of these conversations
usually start with, "Do you still kiss?" I remember being at
a ministry conference where I met a cheerful and outgoing couple
when this question slipped out of my mouth. I'm not sure what I
was expecting, but on this occasion the raw approach blew up in
my face. The couple squirmed, looked at one another, closed their
mouths, then looked right back at me with a sadness you could
cut with a knife. Their silence said it all. *No. We do not kiss. We
are not intimate. We are not happy.*

Ever notice how the Bible describes the intimacy between a
man and a woman? "Adam *knew* Eve his wife, and she conceived..."[1]
Something deep within us longs to be known.

Marriage is not just about marriage. "This mystery is
profound, but I'm saying that it refers to Christ and the church."[2]
It's not like God needed an object lesson to illustrate our
relationship with him so he settled for marriage, since everybody
knows about marriage. Marriage was created to be a sign pointing
to our relationship with God. Which brings us back to our problem.

Too much Christianity is like a travel agent selling timeshares
for a property he's never seen, or a vegan waiter pushing meat
loaf he's never tasted. The pictures look good and the food smells

great, but the experience is second-hand. We really need to stop treating the Bible like a brochure.

Far too many believers are bored with their relationship with God. Like spiritual pornographers, they attend religious gatherings to watch other people encounter God, while they themselves are lifeless and dull, wearied by the "duties" associated with "serving" God. Perhaps their faith is only inferential, the result of a long list of deductions. It is possible to have good theology, do good mission, live a good life, and tell your friends all the good facts about God but still know very little of God.

It is alarming to note just how unimportant the pursuit of God has become to the average Christian. How quickly it drops down the list of priorities. In the light of all the biblical promises and invitations attached to seeking God, how can we explain how unmotivated most believers are to seek the face of God? How easily it gets postponed? How apt we are to call it legalism? Digging always feels like a chore, until you find the buried treasure.

Living *for* God without intimacy *with* God is dead work. Drudgery. This is the problem with natural religion, or natural Christianity, or natural mission. Mission *to* the world without a connection *with* the God who loves the world is a filthy rag, and far too much of our ministry is deprived of the soul-morphing effect of an intimate encounter with God. It's what makes Peter's confession "You are the Messiah, the Son of the living God," so explosive. "Flesh and blood did not reveal this to you..."[3] Have you experienced such *revelation?* There are far too many flesh and blood Christians doing far too much flesh and blood mission that predictably leads to flesh and blood communities. But there is so much more—if we'll dig.

Listen to David: "The intimate friendship of the Lord is reserved for those who fear him, and he makes known to them his covenant."[4] How did he respond? "My eyes are ever towards the Lord."[5] This chapter is a plea to rediscover the difference of a heart fueled by the simplicity of the first love.

Our deepest desire must not be family or ministry or growth or mission or community. We want God. Whatever we do, may it be the result of this experiment: What happens when communities of Jesus-followers set apart their lives to seeking the face of the living God? The outgrowth of that, then, is to seek the lost and the least—a true expression of Church. This is our ultimate dream: to engage in lives and mission *defined by* their pursuit of God himself, so that it is so very clear that He is glorious. This is *primary.* He is our first love.

Often times we seek the fruits and gifts of God in pursuit of fulfillment, but even they never fully satisfy. God's gifts were never meant to substitute for God himself. We are to pray for harvest, innovation, expansion, excellence, provision, creativity, divine appointments, protection, and a million other things, but what we *most* want is God; to know him and to be found in him. Everything else is rubbish in comparison.

We must live—not out of an achiever's need to accomplish, an American need to compete, because it's never been done, or because everybody else is doing it. We are to live the supernatural outgrowth of our relationship, friendship, and intimacy with God. Thus, our primary desire is not for leadership or family or mission; it is seeking and responding to Jesus. We are God-seekers. We must be delivered from the nonsense of "doing our devotions" and all other forms of minimum requirement approaches to seeking God. Our lives are his, and we must gladly set them apart like a living sacrifice.

The world does not need another good church or another interesting missional movement or another nice family or another tribe characterized by good business principles and natural talent. We need something *different.* What we want to bring to the table is an obsession with God that translates into mission inspired by God, which leads us into a truly authentic community. In a world starving for community, the irony is that you never find it by looking for it; you find it by looking for God and then experiencing him with people willing to go there with you.

GOD SEEKING

At the center of our leadership must be the leveraging of every bit of our influence to cause people to seek Him. This is the centrality of our call. We are to make people thirsty enough to drink living water and then mobilize them once they've had a drink. For the unregenerate we call this evangelism, but there is another form of evangelism needed for the believer. We get lost, too. We fall asleep, we grow dry, we lose our way—but because we've done the experiment a thousand times we know this: when we seek God we come back to life.

The promises are magnificent. Our call gets rediscovered in the pursuit of God. Vision becomes sharp in the secret place. Mission comes alive when our hearts are set on seeking him. Leadership is remarkable when the leader brings direction that came from hours spent burning in his presence. Words have authority when the tongue has been silenced in a time of listening. Hope is rekindled, faith is stirred, peace is obtained, promises are embraced, fears are stilled, opposition is exposed. The evidence is astounding: those who make the sacrifice of seeking God inherit promises. Yet therein lies the problem. It is indeed a sacrifice.

Our eternal "position" changes the moment we re-orient our trust. That is, in the moment we turn from our righteousness to His, we shift. We change, are born from above, our slate wiped clean, our adoption is made real. We are seated with Him in heavenly places. When we shift our soul gaze from our goodness (or wickedness) to the greatness of God, we believe. And this eternally life-altering change of orientation makes all the difference in the world as our spirit bows to Jesus.

Yet in the same way that we change *positionally* through regeneration, we have an ongoing need for this same kind of re-orientation *practically*. At the level of activity, attention, and schedule, everything must bow to Jesus. All other activities should take their cue from having first bowed to Jesus. The human soul is a fickle thing. Nothing short of constant and direct abiding, remaining, and communing affords it the ability to maintain a practical freedom from idolatrous tendencies. It is an act of faith to step out and commit time to God with his promise that there is actually nothing in life better than God himself.

For example, the activist disconnected from her Source will indeed work for the afflicted, but she won't be free to truly *serve* them; she will instead *use* them to scratch a personality itch, or worse, establish a deeper self-righteousness. The leader who has left his first love may still work diligently, but won't be alive enough to wash his people's feet; he'll use his position as a stepping stone to build his little kingdom. The father who stops seeking God may continue to love his children, but his love becomes warped; he'll turn his family into a functional idol to fill the void left by an empty throne in his heart. The same can be said of the artist with his art, the entrepreneur with his innovation, or the pastor with his ministry.

It is precisely the first love which orders all the other loves. Which makes the first rebuke in the book of Revelation so painfully relevant: "But I have this against you, that you have left your first love."[6] God forbid! How easy it is to try to fill the needs in our lives with mission or community when it should be filled by God. In those times, the community or mission becomes unhealthy. But when God is first, all the other things fall into place. We may have many loves; but there must be only one *first* love. In our age of rushing and striving and restlessness, we must come out from among them and be holy. We simply must become different.

David had insight into this reality when he penned the words to Psalm 27:

> One thing have I asked of the Lord, that will I seek after: that I may dwell in the house of the Lord all the days of my life, to gaze upon the beauty of the Lord, and to inquire in his temple.[7]

This is the essence of God-seeking: to *gaze* upon his beauty and to *inquire* of his heart. Gazing and inquiring.

When we gaze, we morph. It is one of the pivotal realizations of life: we grow in the direction of our gaze. We become like the things we most deeply behold. This is why the apostle Paul would write, "And we all, with unveiled face, beholding the glory of the Lord, are being transformed into the same image from one degree of glory to another."[8] Transformation is not the result of trying harder; it is the result of beholding more deeply the beauty and weightiness of God.

This has a very concrete application. Many of us have developed a disciplined and effective life of intercession and petition. This is noble and necessary, but should never replace the act of simply being with and worshipping God.

But then we inquire. We open our souls to the Word of God. We receive instruction. We dialogue. We learn. We grow deeper. We run our plans, feelings, and struggles by God. We listen for direction and expect him to enlighten us. We access the mind of Christ. A major agenda in our times alone with God should be to simply gaze, and then to come back and live in the light of the gaze.

SHUT THE DOOR

What does this mean in the real world? This is where the great concrete realist Jesus provides three words that will change everything, if we respond: But when you pray, go into your room and *shut the door* and pray to your Father who is in secret. And your Father who sees in secret will reward you."[9] *Shut the door.*

You might be thinking about how to do such a thing. There's so much to *do.* Isn't there a world to win, darkness to invade, slaves to rescue, justice to work, churches to plant, poverty to address, spouses to love, and families to raise? Yes. There are many things to do *once* we have shut the door, but there might as well be nothing to do *until* we have done so. Don't you see how incredibly foolish it is to spend your life doing things that your Father was never calling you to do? Or doing them in a soul-power you were never supposed to rely upon? How do we change the world? How do we change our lives? It all starts with gazing and inquiring.

We meet Christians all the time who complain about the distance they feel from God. They wonder, "Where is Father?" Yet Jesus tells us where we find him: behind the shut door.

History has not been changed by great people. It's been changed by people who shut the door. It's not amazing people who gaze and inquire; it's when people gaze and inquire that they become amazing. We need microchurch leaders, mothers, activists, and businessmen alike to become obsessed with, and then act upon, these three words: Shut the door.

Have you ever tried to bake a cake with the oven door open? The cake won't rise. The oven produces the heat, but if that heat is allowed to escape, the cake ingredients will not chemically mix. A vacuum cleaner will not work with an opening in the system. The effectiveness of your soul demands the cosmic reality of a holy vacuum behind the shut door. When we gather with our church, engage in mission, and listen to worship music, we get near to the flame, but shutting the door allows us to be shut in completely with the all-consuming fire. This is why we need to live lives of shutting the door. Look closer at what it is Jesus is teaching us.

THE SHUT DOOR GUARDS US FROM HYPOCRISY

> And when you pray, you must not be like the hypocrites. For they love to stand and pray in the synagogues and at the street corners, that they may be seen by others.[10]

Hypocrisy. Everybody hates it, yet we all struggle with it. Nowhere does it show up more than in our spirituality. I sometimes wonder who we are trying to impress. If you're a newer follower of Jesus you may still be uncorrupted, but it doesn't take long to become mildly twisted by some of the public experiences of our spirituality. Take something like corporate prayer. Sometimes it's the awkward moment of waiting for your turn to pray. Should you be listening and agreeing? Should you let others go first or just jump right in? What about corporate worship gatherings? What do you do if you're an extrovert in a room full of introverts? What if you're contemplative and intellectual in a gathering of emotionally-charged but theologically weak worshippers? Are you being fake if you try to "join in?" Are you being a punk if you hold back and do nothing?

The only answer for the pitfalls of the public place is the remedy of the secret place. Jesus gives us the antidote to approval addiction: time alone with Father, behind the shut door. There, we are able to tap into the power of His approval. There, we are free from any necessity to impress anyone. What a difference the shut door makes.

THE SHUT DOOR SAVES US FROM DISTRACTIONS

But when you pray, go into your room and shut the door...[11]

There are so many ways to apply the shut door. Fasting shuts the door on other cravings. Corporate prayer shuts the door on other activity. A secluded location really can shut the door on other noises, and noise is a big deal. Central to our problems lies our propensity toward allowing the noise of this world to drown out the sound of heaven. I find it interesting how Adam and Eve "heard the sound of the Lord God walking in the Garden in the cool of the day."[12] What sort of "sound" did God make? Surely every animal in the Garden rustled the leaves and produced some sort of sound, but I've often wondered what the "sound" of God was like. Was it His voice? Was it a song? Of course we have no idea, but we do know this: the human soul thrives when it lives in the reality of the *sound* of God. Do you recognize the "sound" of God in your life? The shut door has a unique ability to recalibrate a human heart to the sound, voice, and rhythm of God.

This world knocks us off beat. The shut door provides the opportunity to discern again the rhythms of God's grace, and to realign the soul accordingly. It is a pity how much Christian ministry is accomplished out of tune and on the wrong beat. We must reclaim the difference.

SHALLOW WELLS

As Nicholas Carr argues in his intriguing book "The Shallows: What the Internet is doing to our brains," we live in a web based world that has intellectual and certainly spiritual consequences. Our minds are becoming shallow and our relationships increasingly so. Technology is changing us. When you get on a bus, people no longer acknowledge each other; they're plugged in. If you go to a gym, people don't make eye contact; their headphones have them in another world. Even in restaurants, it's not uncommon to see a family of four, sitting silently, each attached to their phones. Fewer and fewer people are reading books. More and more people are having a harder time thinking deeply about things that really matter. Hence the need for sound bites and CliffsNotes arguments. Technology causes us to gaze, and we grow in the direction of our gaze. Our attention spans are shot. Which is quite the problem for the God who calls us to wait.

Our axe heads are dull, and our wells are shallow. Our families live on edge. Our leaders burn out. So much of our work is weak because we never functionally enter into our rest. In a world that worships busyness, rest seems lazy. Even time in prayer seems like we are cheating on life. This leads us to a work mentality. Sometimes we have to put aside our desire to change the world and just let Father change us. He does not pay wages, but He does give rewards. He gives gifts: peace, joy, and gladness. We're always at our best when we live out of the overflow instead of from our reserves.

The 'Secret Place' of time alone with God is the antidote for the obscene pace of life. Our own mind gives us enough reason to be distracted while we seek God. We think about what we will do later, perhaps a bill that needs to be paid or an ache in our little toe. Our phone buzzes, and we look. Distraction. If only we could learn to rest. The Secret Place is like a bite-sized Sabbath.

But you need to shut the door. Turn off the phone. Turn off the computer. Let the kids know 'thou shalt not interrupt.' Forget about the news. Consider the possibility that the world will go on, even if you are unavailable. Your soul needs time each day that is *different*, set apart, off-limits, undivided. I hear Christians throw around the term *quiet time*, but that's not good enough. Your soul needs more than a quiet time, it needs a unique time. Because he is worthy.

But where? If you live with other people, you may not have the ability to lock yourself away for an hour or two. But you can pray in a bathroom. Or in the woods. Or under an apron. Seriously. This is apparently what the godly mother of John Wesley did each day in the middle of her kitchen.

Does it have to be in the morning? Of course not. But even if you are not a morning person, setting your heart and your mind in your relationship with Father before you start your day may be easier than you think. And will give benefits more than you think possible.

And after you have shut the door, *keep the door shut*. Don't leave until you're done. Endure boredom, if necessary. Waiting does what nothing else will do. One of the primary functions of the Secret Place is to deliver us from hurry sickness, attention deficits, and fear. It's all worldliness. Don't be surprised when God's means of deliverance feels like what it is: painful soul-deliverance. Flesh-crucifixion. There really is a threshold in the pursuit of God that, once crossed, makes all the effort worth it. But until that threshold is crossed, so much of the activity of our lives is embarrassingly dull. Beware of doing too much work on the wrong side of the threshold. Beware of attempting crucial conversations on the wrong side of the threshold. Beware of trying to accomplish in natural power what was only meant to be done with the power accessed on the right side of the God-seeking threshold.

Your heart needs to change its gaze to guard you from hypocrisy. Your soul needs to shut the door to save you from your idols.

THE SHUT DOOR LEADS US TO OUR FATHER

We love being fathers. And while we have enjoyed the journey of raising children from the crib all the way to college, there is something precious about that stage when our little ones still act like we walk on water. There is nothing quite like a child who thinks so much of his dad that he tells all his friends about him. Why are they so bold in their bragging and so liberal with their affection? Because they're loved, and they know it. We carry them to bed and we wrestle; we tell them stories and we play. It's first-hand experience. There is a reason we struggle with shutting the door and seeking God. All hell knows the truth: when we seek, we find our Father.

In Romania in 1989 a terrible tragedy in child development came to light. Due to internal strife, there were thousands of abandoned babies who had never known love. These babies had what the medical world calls "failure to thrive." There is no medical explanation for this disorder. It is a lack of emotional security that causes the soul to wither. A life without intimacy with our Father causes us to fail to thrive. Our spirit starves.

The world is in dire need of movements that first shut the door. There will be many doors to open, many injustices to address, and many initiatives to embrace, but not until we have first shut the door. The shut door inspires direction, corrects error, awakens holy ambition, puts to death selfish ambition, and most importantly rekindles the first love.

I spoke with a man recently who came away from a debate with a Christian group. He could not out-talk the Christians, and he did not out-think the Christians. Yet, as I debriefed with him after his encounter, he ended with these words: "I just don't want to be like them."

It is entirely common to watch a Christian begin their race in love and passion, only to drift into the realm of duty and drudgery. Even among the many missional movements popping up left and right, the vast majority reflect the same impatience, self-reliance, and fleshly ambitions of the rest of culture. The shut door has a way of keeping a soul connected with the one thing—the one person—capable of rescuing us in our drift: our Father. This is why the first love is so vital. This is why, the longer you walk with Jesus, the more you wash people's feet by guarding that first love. Duty becomes delight.

We follow Jesus, and he *only did* what he saw the Father doing.[13] How did he know what the Father was doing? Of course he was sinless. Of course he prayed without ceasing, but we would be wise not to neglect details provided at the beginning of his ministry. "And rising very early in the morning, while it was still dark, he departed and went out to a desolate place, and there he prayed."[14] Sounds an awful lot like a "secret place" where he could shut the door on all the other noises of life. To shut the door on distraction. To shut the door on temptation. To shut the door on all competitors for his attention. Behind the shut door the Father gets the monopoly, and that's where we hit the cosmic jackpot.

One of the truly outstanding leaders in the Old Testament was a king named Uzziah. His 52-year reign was exceptional on so many levels. He was an accomplished manager, inventor, and entrepreneur that caused the people of Judah to experience refreshing peace and justice. How do we explain such success? "He set himself to seek God... and as long as he sought the Lord, God made him prosper."[15] That is a verse you can build your life on. God truly is a rewarder of those who diligently seek him.

I'm always convicted when I get to sit in on conversations with godly saints from other countries. "We're in awe of just how much you are able to accomplish—without God." "Why would you say that?" I've asked. Our prayer lives, they explain, tend to reveal our perceived dependence upon God. We're just too strong.

It is for this reason that Uzziah's story does not end well. "He was marvelously helped, until he was strong. But when he became strong, he grew proud, to his destruction."[16] There is only one true antidote for pride. Gazing and inquiring. Shutting the door in order to commune with humility himself. Only one thing shocks us out of our wretched self-reliance and foolish insecurities: the experienced love of our Father.

I (Mike) remember sitting at the dinner table with my children when a strange question came into my mind. *Does Daddy have a favorite child?* To my horror, several of them responded with a yes. Now I was concerned. I paused, and then asked, "Well, who is my favorite?" That's when it happened: all of their hands went up. I was speechless. I am Father's favorite. You are Father's favorite.

This world gets changed by a movement of the first love, but the fuel for first love is to realize you were first *loved.* I hear all these voices telling us we need to know who we are. Yet our chief problem with our identity is our failure to spend enough time with the one person able to speak our identity into the parts of our soul where we need it most. If only you knew how Father feels about you, you'd waste your life in pursuit.

You do not get to choose your IQ, your talents, or your upbringing, but you do get to choose how passionately you seek the face of God. This is a call to make intentional, premeditated, sacrificial commitment to meet God in the secret place. Surely, this is part of what it means for us to be different, set apart, in the world he wants to win through us.

ONE
TWO
THREE
FOUR
FIVE
SIX
SEVEN
EIGHT
NINE
TEN
ELEVEN
TWELVE

Fashion, Trends, and Love for the Poor

*We cannot expect the watching world to listen to our message if
they do not see in our lives the embodiment of that message in
the weakest and the poorest among us. When we love the poor we
not only validate what we say and glorify Jesus, we also welcome
him more deeply into our own lives. The revolutionary choice
that Jesus made to bind himself theologically to the poor means
that our relationship with him is somehow connected to our
relationship with them. To love Jesus is to remember the poor.*

I n March of 2012, a group of young filmmakers set out to make
a short documentary film exposing the war crimes of central
African warlord Joseph Kony. The campaign asserted its goal
was to make Kony famous. They believed (whether rightly or
wrongly) that it was the lack of notoriety and public outcry that
was silently aiding the brutalization of a regime that routinely
killed, maimed, and turned children into soldiers. The film became
the most viral online video ever, amassing 100-million views in
a matter of days, but as the world watched in horror the media
attention began to overwhelm the film's creator, Jason Russell.
His story took a bizarre turn as he had a mental breakdown,
culminating in a naked rant through the streets of San Diego.
The nobility of their cause aside, the fame that was the tool
for the advancement (or rather, awareness) of the project also
became its undoing.

In his first interview after the breakdown, Jason Russell
spoke candidly about the fickle nature of fame and celebrity.
"America loves trends, the danger of making justice a trend is
that it will, by definition fade. It becomes uncool to like a thing

that was cool a month ago." This observation is both important and prophetic. If we live by the media sword, we will die by it as well. If the groundswell of a trend takes your boat up, it will also take it down again, and leave it beached and broken on the shore.

THE FAILURE OF FASHION

If this is the inevitable outcome of trying to leverage a trend to make a point, isn't it irresponsible to take something that is eternally significant and try to package it as cool? Whatever is gained by the initial surge of interest and popularity is more than negated by the hostility that people will soon feel towards it because it is no longer *en vogue*. This is why our work and commitment to the poor and our unflappable commitment to love is best demonstrated when done in obscurity; it can never be something that is degraded to the realm of fashion.

Is concern for the poor a trend? There is little doubt that there has been a renaissance of writing and speaking in recent years on the topic. From my perspective, the concern for justice was followed by a need to act justly in relationship with the poor. This has been followed by a much needed theology of mission for those who began to play in that arena without really understanding the depth and richness of the Biblical choices they were making. Still, the shift to becoming "missional" actually represents a move away from the practicality and specificity of concern for the poor. Caring for the poor has become tired, and the missional framework is both fresh and to some degree relieving. The groundswell of theology calling us to just action and ongoing relationship with the poor has been replaced by a more generic call to just be "missional" anywhere.

This can be conveniently interpreted as serving anyone: the wealthy, our friends, even our own families. The danger however is that this interest first in justice, then the poor, and then missiology meets the same dynamic criteria of a trend. Even though these concepts are eternal, we cheapen them when we reduce them to fashion. The danger of any trend is that the novelty will eventually wear off. If the primary motivation for interest in serving the poor is novelty, then it is doomed to wane in time.

I do not know if there is anything to be done about it; I simply want to expose the dynamic so that when and if the trend abates, we will be ready to persevere with conviction and in so doing distinguish ourselves. Similarly, for those of us who have gotten on this bandwagon there is an implicit warning here to deepen our heart's resolve so that when or if it becomes unpopular to care about the poor, we do not fail the gospel by forgetting them.

The true church was loving the poor before it became popular, and hopefully we will continue after the trend dies down. This is what will make us different; not that we agree with a growing consensus that poverty is a problem, but that we establish ourselves with Isaiah, James, St. Francis, and Dorothy Day in the stream of history saying that poverty is and always has been evil, and we are compelled by love to advocate for those who suffer under its weight. This is the call that we are making; not just to love the poor and the least, but to endure in that love.

Love is not a trend. And love is in its zenith when it is given to the least. Therefore ministry born out of love for the least can never be something we relegate to trend. If Bono cares about the developing world, or Angelina Jolie about orphans, amen, let them join us in a work long labored. It might be cool or it might be uncool, but it should always be at the heart of all we do and all we are. Let us be different in that we are the ones who are already there, already committed and already laying down our lives for the needy and the kingdom that promises them more.

THE FOCUS OF OUR MISSION

We have to rethink what we consider success in ministry. If we think that a big ministry equals a healthy or transformative ministry, we are naive and misinformed. Too many mega-ministries have negligible or no effect on the cities in which they are planted.

How is it that we still consider size the primary measurement for success in ministry? With all the talk of mission and movements (language we both affirm) the metric has now shifted to the size of your network. We ask questions about how many churches one has planted, but if the churches we plant are just as ineffective and self-referential as the churches we started with, then what difference will more make? In other words, one, one thousand, or one million churches that are ineffective will still be ineffective. I honestly wonder if we were to offer the average church leader 10 people who were real disciples or 1,000 that were not, would most take the 1,000?

One of the casualties of this mentality of measurement is that we have to target and accommodate the wrong kind of people. Jesus, who is our model, explicitly exercised a preference in his ministry for the poor. He chose to start with them. His own rationale was that they were the ones that were the most open because they were the ones who understood their need. He always started with the poor, because he believed the kingdom of God belonged to such as these. He had come for them.

If anyone else—a Simon the Pharisee, a rich young ruler, a Levi—would enter the kingdom and choose to follow him, they would have to become like the poor. The poor then are not just the primary target of Jesus' ministry; they become the shapers of its culture. If you wanted to be around Jesus, you had to be willing to also be around lepers and prostitutes and masses of the materially poor. This was among many things that the rich and well adjusted found distasteful about Jesus and his followers. Yet these were the conditions he set for those that would abide in his presence. It is not that Jesus didn't love and welcome the rich. To respond with that kind of defensiveness is to miss the point. Jesus is drawing all of his followers into the heart of mission, redemption, and soteriology itself. There can be no salvation without a crisis of need, without poverty. Jesus comes for those who need, and if we will not be with those people then we cannot be with Jesus.

LOVE BY ASSOCIATION

In perhaps one of the most challenging passages in all of the gospels, Matthew 25 reveals the deliberate theological and relational bond that Jesus makes with the poor:

> Then the King will say to those on his right, 'Come, you who are blessed by my Father; take your inheritance, the kingdom prepared for you since the creation of the world. For I was hungry and you gave me something to eat, I was thirsty and you gave me something to drink, I was a stranger and you invited me in, I needed clothes and you clothed me, I was sick and you looked after me, I was in prison and you came to visit me.' Then the righteous will answer him, 'Lord, when did we see you hungry and feed you, or thirsty and give you something to drink? When did we see you a stranger and invite you in, or needing clothes and clothe you? When did we see you sick or in prison and go to visit you?' The King will reply, 'I tell you the truth, whatever you did for one of the least of these brothers of mine, you did for me.'[1]

If we would love him, we must love them. And when we love them, we are loving him. This text does not deify the poor. The transference is invisible. Both the commended and the judged remark, "When did we see you?"

When we are with the poor, we do not notice Jesus. We see the poor, but there is a supernatural relationship that God has with the outcast, the oppressed, and the forgotten. Even though everyone else abandons them, he never does, and he makes his presence with them not just a reward for those who would love them in his name, but a measurement of judgment for those that continue to obscure them.

If we look at our churches and spiritual communities, are they really places where the poor are sought, nurtured, and welcomed? Or are we trying to grow our ministries by targeting the middle class and the well-adjusted, knowing that they will help us create an environment that will attract other similarly middle class and well-adjusted people?

Almost every church I know has a ministry for children, but how many have showers for the homeless? We serve who we target. We want to be hospitable to parents with children because they have jobs and money and respectability, so we provide childcare. However, if we were targeting the people Jesus targeted (not excluding the middle class) we would be offering a different set of services. Likewise, every church has a nursery, but almost none of those nurseries are set up for special-needs children.

Would the truly poor be welcome in your spiritual community? Would they feel at home? Would there be any services immediately and obviously available and set up for them? Further, are the poor (in any definition you choose) the focus of your work?

The hard word from Matthew 25 is that when we set up churches that neglect or ignore the poor among us, we are actually excluding Jesus himself. We trade the presence and comfort of the middle class for the presence of Jesus.

Conversely, if your ministry does practice hospitality to the poor, making them fit in and feel at home, if your ministry suffers in size because of that, driving away more affluent people, then Matthew 25 is the ultimate consolation. You may not have a ton of people, but you have the presence, pleasure and comfort of Jesus.

Please don't write this text off, or reason it away. Please don't do another injustice to the poor and disservice to the teaching of Jesus by breezing over this. Even as we write this, these words are indictments and profound challenges to us and our ministries. Both of us are deeply committed to the poor and have tried to build our communities around that conviction and still these words set upon us like fire. They are the tenderest of words for the neglected and forgotten and the most tenacious for those of us who are tempted to hide our lives in the values of middle class Christianity instead of the Kingdom of God.

THE LOSS OF CONTROL

A number of years ago, a homeless man stood outside one of our services holding up signs. I only saw him out of the corner of my eye on the way in and didn't pay much attention. I figured someone from our community would likely befriend him and invite him in, which they did. I, on the other hand, was pretty focused (as I usually am) on the talk I was about to give. The text for that morning was Matthew 25. I should also tell you that we had another regular at the time that was homeless who always sat in the front, and on most Sundays, would offer uninvited accompaniment to the band with his harmonica. When he wasn't playing his harmonica (almost never on key) he was shouting along (it was so loud it just couldn't be considered singing). I alternated from week to week on feeling both joy and annoyance at his participation.

I usually sit in the back while the music is going on, and on this day I found myself sitting next to the guy with the signs. Someone had obviously invited him in, assuring him that he was more than welcome, and didn't need to picket our gathering. Still he insisted on holding up his sign during worship. To complicate things he also chose to sing different songs than we were singing and gradually became more than a little distracting to me. I should note that I am easily distracted in these kinds of settings, so instead of joyfully worshiping alongside this stranger, I was fuming. I leaned over and urged him to put his signs down and just enter into worship. He ignored me and just kept on doing his thing. I really struggled with this guy's presence as I considered if I should just ask him to leave. It finally occurred to me to read the sign he was holding, it was an excerpt from Matthew 25.

As I walked to the stage that day, I felt a deep sadness in myself as I realized that the two people who perhaps most embodied Jesus in that audience (one in the front and one in the back) were the two I most wanted to leave. I never preached with more conviction the words of this text, because I knew, as I know now, that in my own heart resides the same exclusivist urge to cater to the predictability and stability of the middle class at the expense of the poor. I know what it feels like to want to make space for more people like me and to leave Jesus on the outside.

I am not saying this is easy. Needy people can be very distracting and extremely complicated to deal with. Making room for them almost always means demolishing simple approaches to most things. When Jesus invites us to love the poor he is inviting us to love *him*, and when he invites us to love him in the face of the most desperate, confused, and troubled, he is inviting us into the depths of real love. He once said if you love those who love you what credit is that to you? Love your neighbor? That is human love, it is the love of reciprocation, but when we are called and urged to love the poor we are being invited into God's kind of love. This is the kind of love that dies for its enemies and serves its adversaries.

I am not saying that the poor are always a problem. On the contrary, because of the sacred presence of Jesus accompanying them, they are ultimately a gift to those who would know them. But the poor are the enemy of comfort and conformity. They will wreck a nicely planned worship service. They will spoil well-drawn out plans and organized lives. Deep friendship with the least of these (like a deep friendship with Jesus) will mean an all-out assault on your desire to control the world around you.

If you have surrendered control of your life and let in one of the least, then you know the comfort of this text. You know what it is like to experience the presence of Jesus in the out-of-control experience of working with really needy people. If on the other hand you find these words a kind of indictment to your brand of Christianity, and you feel you have excluded the awkward in favor of the proper while losing Jesus in the process, these words are an invitation into deeper relationship with Jesus and into the heart of the gospel, which is love.

SACRIFICIAL LOVE

The unmistakable call to sacrificial love in the gospel is an easy argument to make. There are few Christians (or non-Christians for that matter) who would dispute the value and moral significance of love. It is the bit of the Bible that everyone seems to agree on;

the trick is figuring out who we are expected to love. Everyone wants to both love and be loved, but what makes the call to love in Scripture both prophetic and revolutionary is the breadth of the command. The Bible doesn't go out of its way to say love your children because that is natural, but it does go out of its way to say love the fatherless, because loving a child who has no father or mother is a harder matter. We ought to love our friends, no doubt, but Jesus commanded us to also love our enemies. Our love of our neighbor is the bedrock of human society, still Jesus called his followers to love, lead, serve, and teach the people at the ends of the earth. We find it obvious to love people who can benefit us, but what of the truly poor who (it seems) can only take from us? These harder to love people become the ultimate meaning and display of love.

Loving God and loving your neighbor is the heart of the law. It is the basic two-part structure of the ten commandments, but as in so many things, Jesus illuminates a deeper and more profound way. "A new command I give you, love each other as I have loved you."[2] As John reflects in another place, "This is how we know what love is, Jesus Christ laid down his life for us..."[3]

It is in the laying down of our lives for people who do not deserve it, who even betray and reject us, that most demonstrates an understanding of the love of God and a fulfillment of Jesus' command.

So many people are looking for their calling and wondering about God's will for them. When in doubt, just love someone on the margins. This is always God's will. The promise underneath the challenge of Matthew 25 is that he will be with us when we are with the truly needy. If you pour out your life for them, he will be present in the exchange.

Some of us have said yes to this call. Some of us have entered into a relationship with needy people, and if you have, you've likely also experienced both the pain and the beauty of that kind of ministry, but for how long? Too many of our experiences with the poor are short term excursions. We fly into the world of the needy to have an encounter with God and a sobering of our own lives, only to fly out and retreat to the comfort of our middle class sanctuaries. While we are grateful for short term experiences that introduce middle class Christians to the poor, we are compelled to invite you into a deeper kind of love.

PERSEVERING LOVE

Remembered as the first desert father, Anthony was renowned to have said to a young acolyte who asked what he must do to please God, "Always have God before your eyes, whatever you do, do it according to the testimony of the holy Scriptures, in whatever place you live, do not easily leave it. Keep these three precepts and you will be saved."[4] The first two we know, but is staying where you are that important for the spiritual life? G.K. Chesterton said, "There are two ways to come home and one of them is to stay."

One of the most remarkable moments in the discipleship of Peter, James, and John must have been the day that Jesus was transfigured in prayer and appeared with Moses and Elijah. In the narrative of Mark's gospel, this episode happens after the second touch revelation of the cross. In chapter 8, Jesus asks the central Christological question, "Who do you say that I am?"[5] He then answers it by affirming the part they have right and challenging the part they have wrong. "He then began to teach them that the Son of Man must suffer many things and be rejected by the elders, the chief priests, and the teachers of the law, and that he must be killed and after three days rise again."[6] He took this troubling revelation even further saying, "Whoever wants to be my disciple must deny themselves and take up their cross and follow me." This is the part where it is no longer cool to follow Jesus. Any self-interest is quickly ferreted out by his prediction of a destiny that always finds its way to death. And the remarkable part is that they don't leave. Their perseverance and love is rewarded as six days later Jesus is transfigured before them. Not just because they agreed once on a shore in Galilee to *follow* him, but because they *abided* with him. Jesus called and they answered, but each day they renew that answer in their staying. They were promised suffering, but six days later they see the face of the patriarchs, hear the voice of God, and discover the truth about Jesus. They get to see the deeper secret he was keeping, because they said yes to go, and yes to stay.

We follow because of our own hopes and expectations, but we stay because we find him to be God. You don't know if you have really put your faith in the real Jesus until you have felt the weight of a cross and the burden of persevering love. It is conjecture to guess what the disciples were really thinking or expecting when Jesus first called them, but perhaps it is not far from what we were expecting. What they heard in the first call was, "Follow me," but they almost certainly filled in the rest on their own:

Follow me... and you will be happy.
Follow me... and you will be somebody.
Follow me... and you will be the center of attention.
Follow me... and you will have the perfect family.
Follow me... and everything will go well for you.

But then the following becomes real. It moves from the romantic notions of the mind to the stark naked reality of practice. And the illusionary second half is replaced by the truth:

Stay with me... and you will deny yourself.
Stay with me... and you will die.
Stay with me... and you will be nobody, obscure.
Stay with me... and you will walk with sinners and the poor.

But if you can do that, if you can persevere, then you will see life from death and wonders beyond your wildest dreams. Anybody is up for an adventure, but it is the perseverance that makes us different.

At the time of writing both of us have been married about 20 years, and we can definitively say that a marriage is not defined by the wedding. Marriage is in the fights, the health struggles, the tragedy, the failed expectations, and the forgiveness. We do not vow to vow, we vow to stay. What makes the vow of a wedding weighty is not the vow to love but to *persevere* in that love. That's what makes the vow have power. That's what love is. Can you imagine if people entered into a marriage based on how they would really live, or how we enter into ministry work, or how too many of us have entered into care for the poor?

Do you take this woman to be your wife?
To have and to hold... until you find something better?
Or until it gets worse?
Or until she gets sick?
Or until it gets hard?
Or until she fails you in some way?
Or until the money runs out?
Or until you just otherwise get tired of her?
Untill boredom, or frustration, or anything uncomfortable do you part.

What have we learned in 40 years of combined marriage? It is in the staying that greatness is gained, in the keeping of the vow, not in the making of it. Here is the good news: what is gained in the staying is so beautiful, so tangibly magnificent, that it is all worth it. This is the implicit promise of Jesus. If you will stay another six days, then you will see wonders beyond your wildest dreams. This is the promise of persevering love.

A church made up of Christians who refuse to love the unloved, give a voice to the voiceless, and provide a place for the displaced is never going to win the watching world. No level of performance excellence will replace the meek beauty and moral authority that is ours when we care for the people that no one else wants. We simply have to be different in this way, or we cannot realistically (or morally) expect the unbelieving world to respect us and listen to our message. Nothing has hurt our witness so much as our lack of love.

Loving the unloved will not be easy, and it will not be glamorous. Like most things worth doing, the life of love can be arduous and deeply painful, but when we persevere in that kind of love, when we walk with the poor and intertwine our lives, when we stand in solidarity with them and their struggle for sanity, dignity, and salvation, we discover the rare, priceless pearl of the kingdom which is Jesus himself, and we finally find ourselves understanding what Paul discovered, "Love never fails."[7]

ONE
TWO
THREE
FOUR
FIVE
SIX
SEVEN
EIGHT
NINE
TEN
ELEVEN
TWELVE

Egomaniacs and the Authority of the Servant

The world will watch the way we handle and apply authority. It is both important and dangerous, for we cannot lead and teach without it, but if we misuse it we betray the message we profess. Authority in the church must come from intimacy with God and true servanthood. Holy leadership will be done by small people who know how to serve and never compete as potential rivals to the beauty, glory, and leadership of God in the lives of those they lead.

Years ago I (Brian) sat on a church leadership team that was led by a pretty humble and hungry older man. All of our people were really impressed with him and although I was busy in campus ministry I agreed to join the teaching team for the church and be involved with the life and decision-making of the staff. Sometime later that leader sensed a call to leave for another church in another state. We blessed him on his way, but it left a big hole in the team.

The church leadership scrambled to fill the spot, and as is often the case in these situations, wrestled with whether to hire someone from the outside or to promote from within. They chose a gifted, creative, and wonderful guy who was already a part of the team. I really enjoyed this guy but knew he did not have the gifts, capacity, or calling to lead. Still, what could I do? I supported this leader for months, watching him flounder in a role that required skills he did not have, and pushed him into complexity he could not understand. At first we grieved for him, trying to support him as people left in protest, or as important responsibilities were neglected. Finally, after weeks of wrestling with what to do, I took a chance and tried to confront him.

THE ENMITY OF EGO AND AUTHORITY

I really liked this man. I believed in his part to play in the kingdom, but everyone could tell this was not it; so I pleaded with him. I asked him if he was feeling overwhelmed by the job. He said yes. I asked if he often felt confused and unsure about what to do. He said yes. I asked if he was happier and had a better relationship with God in his previous role. He said yes. I asked him if he was more committed to the kingdom and to Jesus than to his own advancement or his own position. He said yes. And then I asked him to step down. I laid out a plan that I thought the church would support, for him to keep working and leading, but in a different capacity. Since I had nothing to gain or lose by giving him this advice, I argued that I was trying to serve him and the whole body. In tears, he agreed that it was the right thing to do.

Sadly, his conviction was short lived. The next day he changed his mind. Redoubling his efforts to grow the church, I could not stay to watch. I had taken a stand and tried to stand by it. Within six months, my friend was fired and left the ministry. Since then he has lost his family and is still not fully recovered.

What is it inside us that will not let go? Why are we so unwilling to accept a demotion as the intelligent, strategic, and gracious work of God? I will never know my friend's true motivation, and I don't tell that story to castigate him specifically, but his story makes me wonder why we do ministry in the first place. What moves us to it?

That story has made me ask the question, would I go backwards? If I knew it was best for the kingdom, would I give up influence or authority for the sake of serving Jesus and the people he loves? What do we really want? Do we really want what we pray? For his kingdom to come, for his name to be known, and for the nations to find joy in him? Or do we want our thing to succeed, our name to be spoken, and our ministry or work to be a success?

God is not good with rivals. He just doesn't like them. I am convinced that most ministries don't grow more because of the pride ceiling that their leadership has built into them. In other words, God might love you *too much* to let your ministry grow if it will go to your head and damage your soul.

AUTHORITY AND FRIENDSHIP WITH GOD

It is hard not to look with awe at the life of John the Baptist. The first page of the gospel story is really the last of his own, and while we know a little about his radical prophetic call from the wilderness and his courage to speak truth to power, we also see that he was a man without ego and (in the view of Jesus) a man without equal. [1]

Once this most famous spiritual leader of his time sees that Jesus is moving into public ministry, John immediately instructs his followers to transfer their allegiance to Jesus. He steps from the public eye into obscurity, eventually finding himself alone in prison awaiting his own death. It was in that place of waiting that he confirmed the depth of his own character. "I must decrease so that he may increase."[2] He knew he should not stand as a potential rival to Jesus. He knew that his death was the ultimate sacrifice (one he was willing to make) in order to assure that no one would ever confuse him with Jesus.

Jesus does not call us to eclipse him in the lives of those he comes to save. We are meant to be recipients and servants of his gospel and to serve at his pleasure. Certainly then, some of us might be called into paid service, and some of us, from time to time, out of it. What is the problem with that? Leaving paid ministry does not have to represent a spiritual demotion; if it is done in obedience then it is to be applauded.

Churches don't exist to give jobs to pastors or staff, or to make insecure leaders feel important or to feel as if they have something in their lives they can control. Leadership in the church cannot and should not be confined to people who receive pay. The church is not ours. It is not ours to lead, control, exploit, or cannibalize. It belongs to Jesus. The church is his bride, not ours.

THE LOVE TRIANGLE

When John and his followers wrestled with his place in the story of the coming of the Messiah, he chose the metaphor of the friend of the groom. This is still the best metaphor for us to understand our role as leaders within the church. We are the friends of the groom. Therefore our joy is accomplished in the coming together of the bride and the groom. Our primary relationship is actually with the groom, not the bride. The Christian leader's love and allegiance is to the groom, and because of that love he cares for, serves, and protects the bride. But the bride is not his to possess or control.

Think of two best friends. One falls in love. The ring is bought, the wedding set. But the groom has an assignment with his job that sends him overseas. He can communicate with his bride over email or occasional phone calls but the nature of his job is such that traveling back to help with wedding details and even some of his future bride's needs is just impossible. He is, of course, distraught at not being able to be there to help her with the wedding preparation or her day-to-day struggles. Always weighing on him is the nagging sense that he cannot really look after her or protect her until he returns. So he engages his best friend. "Help me bro. Keep an eye on her, make sure she's okay. Make sure nothing happens to her, and if there is anything she needs, try and help her. As I would."

And so he does. At first for his friend, but then over time, something happens between the friend of the groom and the bride. The groom is mentioned less and less, and the relationship is less and less about the groom and more about them. Until one day the friend realizes he is in love with the bride, with the way she makes him feel. Important, strong, helpful, handsome, and so on, and worse even still, she is in love with him. She has forgotten the groom, and now loves the friend of the groom more. She has come to trust him and rely on him, and the intimacy that was meant for the groom has been stolen by the friend. This is a broken picture of ministry, counseling, discipleship, and more. It is a broken picture of leadership that loses sight of its rightful place.

We meet with a lot of people who want to work with us or align themselves with us in some way. Although we have different kinds of ministries, we both need to be able to tell relatively quickly if we have some kind of chemistry or affinity with someone. We both use the same test. We look to see, if in the course of a meeting about ministry, the person will mention Jesus. You would be shocked how often Christian leaders don't. Even when we bring up Jesus, the subject is too often changed back to ministry. Does this person have a genuine relationship with the groom or just a creepy relationship with his bride to be?

STOP BEING A THIRD WHEEL

It is a warning for those of us who do ministry, who spend a lot of time with the bride, to keep our friendship with the groom strong. To make sure that our primary relationship with him is actually stronger than it is with the bride. Making sure our loyalty to him, to loving him, to serving him, to pleasing him, and to seeing him united with his bride, is more important than accolades or prominence.

It seems the greater the gifts, the greater the honor that a leader receives, the harder this test is. There should be direct correlation between influence and personal depth with God. Too often that correlation is reversed (to disastrous effect) when leaders grow in influence and drift from the God that gave it to them.

Our real job as missionaries, as sent ones, is to see people fall in love with Jesus, not us. We may make the introduction, but then we must be willing to decrease in their lives so that he might increase. It still applies. Our first ambition should be to grow in our love and obedience to the one who first saved and called us. Sometimes our ambition leads our prayers in the wrong direction as we pray to do mission better, forgetting that it is relationship with Jesus that compels us into mission in the first place. Yes, it is that relationship that will sustain us through mission—but actually that relationship is the transcendent part. It is not just the *fuel* to do mission, it is the goal of mission. We are serving the bride in order to draw closer to the groom.

We should do mission because we are in love with Jesus, because we have experienced his grace and want others to experience the same. But if we forget that first love, we ourselves become again the objects of mission.

Prayer is not then a technique for better life or successful ministry. It is the language of our first and most profound love relationship. It is the fire that burns in the heart because the chief end of man is to glorify God and enjoy him forever. And it's all too much for us anyway. Everything that ministry requires is simply beyond us. How can you survive? As a ministry leader I am expected:

To be the ideal father, who has special time with all my kids, throws the ball with my boys, helps with homework, goes to all the recitals and games, never neglecting their spiritual lives, leading in family prayer and bible study times.

To be the perfect husband, who spends lots of time listening, affirming, and serving his wife. Has date night every week, remembers all the small things and the big, makes time for romantic getaways, and remembers to celebrate the everyday.

To be a good son and brother, who always remembers to call (just because), remembers all birthdays, and makes it to all the important family occasions.

To be a good friend and community member, who night or day is available to my friends for counsel or support or to help with a project they need done.

To be a good pastor/shepherd, who responds to every

email, to be there in every crisis or loss or celebration... for *every* person who looks to me.

To be a shining example of mission, keeping strong relationships with non-believers, cross-cultural friendships, relationships with the poor and needy, giving them all my best, my time, and energy.

To be a good executive leader, providing foresight and visionary leadership for our staff, keeping them all inspired and well managed. Writing healthy policies, keeping a disciplined, focused, and professional staff team while paying them very little money.

To be a good elder, a good teacher and preacher, spending hours a week in prayer and preparation.

To be a good fundraiser, entrepreneur, global partner, planter, writer, speaker and collaborator for other ministries.

To not neglect my health, keeping a garden where I raise my own food, exercising and staying in shape, remaining mentally sharp, keeping up with current events, politics, reading dozens of books, as well as pop culture realities like the latest movie or television series...

But how can a person do all that? Won't we go crazy trying, or worse, succumb to self-righteousness if we somehow succeed?

You know how I survive? I do not see my life as plates to spin, or convictions to live, or people to satisfy. That is all just too much. I boil the whole of my life down to this: following Jesus and being a friend of the groom. The result of that kind of clarity is that Jesus can lead me from day to day to be with some of those people, to serve and remember some of those things, and at the end of the day, I can ask myself the only question that matters: Have I been faithful to Him today?

Sometimes that means my children are the focus of my obedience to him, other times it is work, other times it is standing with a grieving friend, a marriage that is buckling, or a skeptic who is wrestling with honest questions. Each of these is as valid as the other, each is exclusive for that moment, and each is the same if it is the assignment God is giving. The distinction between the mundane and the holy, between competing values or priorities, is superseded by the singular call to hear and obey the voice of the one to whom we belong. There is perfect clarity and order to a life abandoned to Jesus and his leadership. The work then is in hearing, in drawing close enough from day to day to listen, and by faith to obey. Our lives are not our own, therefore intimacy is everything. The further you are from the one who has purchased your life, of whom you are but a servant, the more confused and cluttered your life will seem. Besides, you will not be able to bear the burdens of the bride without the provision of the groom.

Too many of us in leadership discover this too late. There is a burning clarity that comes to the seasoned leader who finally surrenders to the supremacy of God in their ministry. We have seen it more than once. Leaders who finally understand they control very little and surrender to that truth (and to the one who controls) find the key to the lucid joy that ministry can offer. They resonate with the tardy but profound realization of Augustine:

> Too late have I loved you, O Beauty of ancient days, yet ever new! Too late I loved you! And behold, you were within, and I abroad, and there I searched for you; I was deformed, plunging amid those fair forms, which you had made. You were with me, but I was not with you. Things held me far from you—things which, if they were not in you, were not at all. You called, and shouted, and burst my deafness. You flashed and shone, and scattered my blindness. You breathed odors and I drew in breath—and I pant for you. I tasted, and I hunger and thirst. You touched me, and I burned for your peace.[3]

True spiritual authority comes from God and is given to those who spend time in his presence. There are no shortcuts to real authority; it is earned through faithful service, granted by the God from whom all authority is derived, and confirmed by the people we have first served.

AUTHORITY IS GIVEN TO THE SELFLESS AND THE SERVANTS

Movements are born in the hearts of selfless leaders; it is an egoless enterprise. Many of our friends are inspired by church planting, others one-up them by planting networks of churches, and the most ambitious will aspire to planting movements. But movements by definition cannot be led, and they cannot be planned. They defy control and a singular identity. A movement is an egoless enterprise. If a movement happens, it will happen because leaders' names are forgotten and no one person or team gets the credit. It must grow out of control. Leaders who aspire to see a movement started, but who are not *also* ready to abandon their own promotion and fame, are incompatible. One must give way to the other. Simply put, a movement is something God must do, and we must decrease in order to see him increase.

People went into the wilderness to see a man like John because he was not a "reed swaying in the wind," but because he was the strongest kind of man. He was someone who could give up his own name, ego, and enterprise when we he was in the presence of someone greater. There was a fierce and fearless strength in the life of John the Baptist, and yet when the defining moment of his life came it was humility that was the greatest display of his strength.

THE SERVANT OF THE BOAT

C.S. Lewis lamented, "Pride leads to every other vice. It is the complete anti-God state of mind."[4] Chesterton quipped, "The chivalrous lesson of 'Jack the Giant Killer'; that giants should be killed because they are gigantic. It is a manly mutiny against pride as such."[5] The tower of Babel was not a marvel of human innovation; it was a challenge to the supremacy and leadership of God. The absence of humility in Christian leaders is an epidemic poisoning the church and all her endeavors. Giant churches, with giant, larger-than-life leaders leading from giant egos, are creating giant structures that must be felled if the kingdom is going to come. This may sound harsh, but we believe that even big churches can be small and that even great ministries can be led by small leaders who make room for God by making room for others. Ironically, great leaders make themselves small so that God is big.

As people interested in leadership and the unique beauty of a team in sync with itself and its purpose, crew is a fascinating sport to consider. A team of rowers is a picture of elegant teamwork and the beauty of a community in sync with itself and its purpose. In crew the rowers face away from the direction they are rowing, leaving the coxswain alone in the back of the boat, facing forward, calling out the cadence for the rowers' rhythm. This is a poignant image for leadership in the church.

Even the name carries etymological significance as it is a compound word, combining cox (boat) with swain (boy or servant). The coxswain is the servant of the boat. In one sense, he or she is the leader. They are the one keeping the team in time, seeing the way forward and even steering the boat with a small rudder at the back. But consider this kind of leadership.

The coxswain sits small in the boat. Since he does not row, great size would only be a liability for the coxswain. The bigger the coxswain, the slower the boat will go. Not only must he be light, he should sit low and stay small in the boat. Crouching to reduce drag, you would never see him sitting up or doing anything to slow the boat down. After all, he is the servant of the boat, playing his part to help it move through the water as fast and directly as possible.

The coxswain calls the rhythm. His voice is critical as he calls the cadence for the rowers to stay on beat. He has to be able to keep that beat, never deviating. He has to be good at this role, or else he should be rowing.

The coxswain sees and steers. His sight is important because no one else is facing forward; they are all relying on his view of the path ahead, the distance left to travel, and their relative position to the other boats. The coxswain serves the boat by keeping his eyes on the finish line; his perspective and placement makes him the eyes of the whole team. While he is not the source of the movement or the power in the boat, he does hold in his hand a small rudder that steers the boat toward or away from its goal.

The coxswain motivates and communicates. Besides seeing just the finish line, the coxswain sits in the privileged position of being able to see the faces of the rowers. He can see the pain, struggle, and discouragement on their faces—and the only face they see is his. He is responsible for their courage. His voice can keep them going.

The coxswain leads from the back, not the front. The leader on a crew team then, is nothing like the image of leadership we stubbornly hold on to. He sits in the back of the boat, as its servant. He does have a unique and specific role, but that role is not *more* significant, it is *less*. He understands his place is at the back of the boat where he can see his team, leaving him as the last person to cross the finish line.

This represents not just our hope for ourselves as leaders, but what we consider a sublimely biblical image of Jesus' leadership paradigm. Servants of the boat sit small and weigh down their people as little as possible, keep their eyes on the future and their teammates' faces, urge them forward while caring about their condition, and steer only so those they serve can cross the finish line first. This is selfless, Christ-like leadership.

Instead, we have permitted the propagation of overweight leaders of the boat. We have allowed our leaders to sit at the front of the boat, facing forward but not facing their people, eager for personal gain and success. These boatmen use the rowers as the engine for their personal vision, fame, and aggrandizement, and it is a scandal. It is not just bad leadership. It is bad *discipleship* and many of the churches who suffer under these kinds of leaders have done so for years. Young, impressionable disciples watch and learn a false model from their predecessors, tragically repeating what they have seen. These young misled disciples wrongly assume that great leaders lead from a stage—at the head of the boat—and not in the background for the sake of the boat.

THE PERFORMANCE IMPERATIVE

In his book *The Death of Character,* University of Virginia professor James Davison Hunter observes that culturally we have changed who we grant the status of celebrity. He recounts a time when celebrity was rewarded for achievement. People were well known because they had accomplished something that distinguished them. Now, celebrity is more often granted to performers, not achievers.[6] People are well known because they can perform or entertain us. This is true in sports, film, music, and even in the church. We no longer look for our leaders to be men and women whose character is forged through years of faithful service to the people of God. Instead, we are drawn to leaders who can perform on stage. The largest churches are not led by the most accomplished leaders, they are led by the best performers.

Missiologically this has been devastating. The church in the west has never been less effective or less potent as salt and light in the world. We are reminded of Jesus' words, "The kingdom of God does not come by your careful observation..."[7] The kingdom will not—and cannot—come through spectating. The kingdom is not a spectacle, and no matter how large a crowd we gather to watch, still it will not come. Instead Jesus said, "It comes by force." Exertion, effort, blood, sweat, and tears.

Imagine a massive boulder, representing all the evil in the world. No matter how large a crowd we draw to watch the boulder, to mock, ridicule, or decry the boulder, it will not move. Some of our churches may have gotten bigger, but those exerting force have gotten smaller and the church is not moving the boulder. When the church has been led by performers and not laborers, when it has been led by charisma instead of servanthood, it has failed to mobilize the real power of the church which is Jesus in his people. In spite of all the resources, large churches tend to be less effective (per capita) in evangelism and discipleship,[8] but it does not have to be that way. Even large churches with charismatic communicators can still make themselves small. Servant leadership is the key.

THE NATURE OF JESUS AND THE NATURE OF GOD

One of the most theologically important texts in all of Scripture, Paul calls us as disciples and leaders to consider the revelation of Jesus' life as a model for our own:

> Do nothing out of selfish ambition or vain conceit, but in humility consider others better than yourselves. Each of you should look not only to your own interests, but also to the interests of others. Your attitude should be the same as that of Christ Jesus: Who, being in very nature God, did not consider equality with God something to be grasped, but made himself nothing, taking the very nature of a servant, being made in human likeness. And being found in appearance as a man, he humbled himself and became obedient to death— even death on a cross! Therefore God exalted him to the highest place and gave him the name that is above every name, that at the name of Jesus every knee should bow, in heaven and on earth and under the earth, and every tongue confess that Jesus Christ is Lord, to the glory of God the Father.[9]

Still, we do not just learn about the nature of leadership or even the virtue and beauty of humility; we learn something shocking about God himself. The theological hand grenade here has to do with the forms that Jesus contains within himself. On the one hand, he was in being, "very nature God." Something the Nicene Creed would render "very God of very God." And on the other hand, he became "the very nature of a servant." Begging the question; can God take on a nature that is contrary to his own? If, for instance, God is in nature good, can he take on the nature of evil? Or if God is, in very nature, honest, can he take on the nature of dishonesty? Certainly not. Whatever is in that nature of God is immutable and certain.

So what then of these two natures of Jesus? If God cannot take on a nature contrary to his own, we are amazed to learn that servanthood is then not contrary to his nature. It is a part of it. God is a servant.

Compound this bombshell with the word *doulon* which is usually rendered servant, but could just as easily be rendered slave. To think of God as slave, bends the mind but also awakens the soul. It does not diminish God, nothing in his nature can, but it does irrevocably elevate servanthood. To serve then, to make the needs of another more important that your own, is a part of the nature of God. But who does Jesus serve? He takes the nature of servant to whom? To people? To God? Or to both?

Juxtaposed in the character of God is both servanthood and rulership. On the one hand we can say that God, by definition is no one's slave. He is a ruler and a leader. And yet on the other hand it is not against God's nature to become Jesus, the empty, humble, servant leader.

AUTHORITY IS GIVEN TO SERVANT-FIRST LEADERS

Consider this second passage where Jesus directly talks about leadership or how to rule:

> Also a dispute arose among them as to which of them was considered to be greatest. Jesus said to them, "The kings of the Gentiles lord it over them; and those who exercise authority over them call themselves Benefactors. But you are not to be like that. Instead, the greatest among you should be like the youngest, and the one who rules like the one who serves. For who is greater, the one who is at the table or the one who serves? Is it not the one who is at the table? But I am among you as one who serves. You are those who have stood by me in my trials. And I confer on you a kingdom, just as my Father conferred one on me, so that you may eat and drink at my table in my kingdom and sit on thrones, judging the twelve

tribes of Israel. "Simon, Simon, Satan has asked to sift you as wheat. But I have prayed for you, Simon, that your faith may not fail. And when you have turned back, strengthen your brothers.[10]

Servant leadership is not just doing what the people you lead want or being a slave to their whims. Servant leadership is not weak because it requires tremendous strength. Jesus was a servant to God first. It is his Father's wishes that come first.

Think of a butler serving a master with guests in the house. The butler serves the guest of the master because the guests are in the graces of the master, but as soon as the wishes of the guest contradict the wishes of the master, the butler will not serve those wishes.

Jesus takes the nature of a servant. He is a leader who becomes a servant who becomes a leader again. This is the flow of Philippians 2. But what are we? We are servants first. We are servants who can become leaders. If we would lead in the kingdom, we have to first acknowledge that we are servants who lead, not leaders who serve. The order matters.

If we are leaders who serve, then it is only a tool or a tactic that we think will help us lead. But if we are servants who lead, then we lead because we are told to. We are leaders who are always conscious that we are under another. When we are servants first, the goal is not leadership, it is obedience and pleasing the one we serve. And we cannot do that, ultimately, unless we become (as he says) "the servant of all." Jesus was a servant of God who became the servant of all. We too must become the servant of all those we lead and are called to.

We need servants who emerge as leaders, not leaders who we teach to serve as a means to an end. This generation is possibly only going to be led by servants, not leaders who fake it.

The seminal book on servant leadership was largely ignored by the church when it was first published in the turmoil of the 1960's. Robert Greenleaf's *Servant Leadership* has stood the test of time and still echoes in this generation an almost prophetic call to servant first leadership. Talking about the new generation of followers on the horizon of that time he wrote, "They will not casually accept the authority of existing institutions. Rather, they will freely respond only to individuals who are chosen as leaders because they are proven and trusted as servants."[11]

ELEVATING SMALL LEADERS

In our own leadership pipelines, we have made the choice to promote proven servants. We do not want to build with gifted leaders (teaching them to serve like Jesus), but instead to build with gifted servants, teaching them to lead like Jesus. It is a question of preeminence and weakness. There should be a spiritual protocol, elevating humility, faithfulness, and servanthood as the necessary qualifications for anyone who would aspire to leadership in the kingdom.

Servant-first leaders become small in the boat because they see themselves as the servants of the boat. They would not dream of doing anything to slow the boat down or to hinder the success of their team. This kind of ruthless altruism must become ordinary in the church again. We must insist on leaders who put the needs of their people before their own, and who refuse with relentless conviction to exploit their people in any way. Ultimately this is a call to leaders to re-envision the nature of their work as servants, but it is also a call to followers to refuse to follow ego-driven, exploitive leaders. The church must become small again as it is led by small leaders who make room for God and others in their presence.

C.S. Lewis, in a reflection on the omnipresence of God, mused that God is not present in the way we are. When we are in a place, we exclude another from that place. If we are in the chair, then no one else can be. God, however, can be present in a place while also making room for someone else to be in that same space. He can be in the chair with us. This is the urge and desire of a servant leader. Big leaders make no room for anyone else. They take up all the space. Small leaders, on the other hand, can be present without excluding the presence of others. In that way they reflect the paradox of God, who is both great and small.

Like the themes before it, leadership and authority have to be handled differently if we are to be taken seriously as agents of God's kingdom. Most people have a general cynicism about authority in this world. Too often the church has done nothing to contrast that mistrust. We simply must produce different leaders who offer a different kind of leadership that illuminates the greatness, of the smallness, of the holiness of God.

ONE
TWO
THREE
FOUR
FIVE
SIX
SEVEN
EIGHT
NINE
TEN
ELEVEN
TWELVE

"WHO IS GREATER, THE ONE AT THE
TABLE OR THE ONE WHO SERVES?"

LUKE 22:27

Visions and Empowered Love

*"This is to my Father's glory, that you bear much fruit, showing
yourselves to be my disciples. "As the Father has loved me,
so have I loved you. Now remain in my love. If you keep my
commands, you will remain in my love, just as I have kept my
Father's commands and remain in his love. I have told you
this so that my joy may be in you and that your joy may be
complete. My command is this: Love each other as I have loved
you."[1]*

Whenen we think about love, we tend to think about
warmth, affection, and kindness. Usually for us, love
is sentimental. Love is an emotion. At times we talk
about it as if it were almost involuntary, like we are victims of
love. "What can I do? I love him." It is tormenting at times, like
Romeo and Juliet; Shakespeare said they "suffered love" for one
other. It is an action too, but born from the heart, the place where
we feel and then do. Love is our most tender word; reserved for
the things we care most deeply about. It is not a word we use
in business or politics. It is more private because love is deeply
personal to us. We love what we love, and in that way, love is
one of the most cherished, but also privatized, virtues. How could
this concept be so central and revolutionary to the core teachings
of Jesus? How is so much of Jesus' teaching summarized by this
simple word?

If you had to describe a coin to someone how would you do
it? Would you only describe the design and image of a single side?
Or wouldn't you describe both sides while also explaining that by
nature a coin is two sided?

POWER AND LOVE

Here the practical theology of people like Paul Tillich and Martin King becomes helpful as they offer an understanding of love that is defined also by power. That love is a coin with two sides, and they argue (compellingly) that real love is only possible when it is accompanied by power, and power is only holy when it is accompanied by love. King said:

> One of the great problems of history is that the concepts of love and power have usually been contrasted as opposites— polar opposites—so that love identified with the resignation of power, and power with the denial of love. Now we've got to get this right. What we need to realize is that power without love is reckless and abusive and love without power is sentimental and anemic. It is precisely this collision... which constitutes the major crisis of our time.[2]

Tillich defined love and power as unity. "To see love, power, and justice as true symbols of the divine life, means to see their unity."[3] He called love "The reunion of the estranged... love manifests its greatest power there where it overcomes the greatest separation."[4] For Tillich, love is an expression of power to reunite; it is the attempt to bring together that which is broken, fractured, and separate. It is reconciliation, and it is the hope of the kingdom. Power is the attempt to realize ourselves, the assertion of our autonomy. Power is the movement to satisfy something in us personally, at times something we want, but more than that, something that we think is important to us. The problem is that these two concepts have been divorced from one another in practice, in ideation, and in theology, like God makes a choice to either exercise power or love, but not both at the same time. In Jesus, we see a new definition of love that is pregnant with power, revealing mirror realities that validate each other's significance. What Jesus calls love is power, too.

Any serious student of the passion narrative will not be able to characterize the cross as an act of powerlessness or passivity.

He does not give in or give up. Will an honest reading lead us to the conclusion that Jesus was overpowered by the Romans, the Jewish ruling class, or the devil? In all the accusations of his trial and execution, one of the only comments he felt compelled to correct was Pilate's plain and pressing statement that he had the power to take Jesus' life from him. Pilate didn't know Jesus had already explained, "I lay down my life—only to take it up again. No one takes it from me, but I lay it down of my own accord. I have authority to lay it down and authority to take it up again."[5] Rarely have we witnessed a greater act of naked strength. No, this is not defeat, it is both a deliberate act of raw power and tender love. What, then, is the implication for those of us who do ministry, for those of us who would bear the fruit of love?

There is no doubt that love characterized the ministry and leadership of Jesus. But perhaps not in the sentimental way we imagine it. Any conception of his loving leadership must also include an equal quotient of power. Jesus was surrendered but never passive; the way he loved people was deliberate and in full awareness of the sacrifices he was making. Even at the cross Jesus was not a victim. He was a savior. His death is the penultimate leadership gesture, and it was a spectacular display of both love and power. He does not call us to power (directly) but to love, because this kind of love—greater love—is conscious of its power. It is ripping you from the grip of death, prying open the long shut gates of hell, winning for you an emancipation from an ancient slavery. Even greater than Solomon's sentiment, it is a love that is stronger than death.[6] For, as Tillich puts it, "Love destroys, as its strange work, what is against love."[7]

Whether leading a company, a church, a home group, or even our families, our leadership must be strong, self-aware, and always sacrificial. We put the needs of others before our own because we understand sacrificial love is true love. We do not seek suffering, but we do not run from it either as we should be people who have counted the cost of leadership and who stand resolute in our will to love. We are willing to suffer for love, and this is the best kind of leadership. It is strong in a way that is unfamiliar to the world—and too often the church. We offer the world a different kind of leader who is neither weak nor self-centered.

LOVE AS WAR

When an infection enters the body, every cell is threatened. Almost miraculously, there are separate sets of cells in our bodies that make up what is called our immune system. Some of these cells are called B cells. Their particular job is to make antibodies that confront antigens, dangerous foreign substances that enter the body. B cells are tough, and they quietly fight off every infection that our bodies face. In every case (that does not end in our death), these little warriors are strong enough to preserve us and to destroy the threat to our health.

Love makes us B cells for the world. We are meant to fight for healing and holiness against the threat of evil with the weapon of empowered love. At every social level, Jesus' people should be offering this subtle resistance to evil. From parents, to teachers, to business owners, and church leaders, everyone who is a disciple of Jesus has this revolutionary assignment from God to love the world toward redemption.

Too often our leaders have been a part of the infection and not the solution. At best, we have called a truce with the evil in our cities, setting small goals of growing our church, or ministry and not fighting for actual transformation. Consider Paul: "For though we live in the world, we do not wage war as the world does. The weapons we fight with are not the weapons of the world. On the contrary, they have divine power to demolish strongholds."[8] This is the work of love; it is divinely empowered to destroy all that is *not* love.

Cycling coach Sir David Brailsford, known for his success with the previously undecorated British national cycling team, has argued that world-class performance is possible when we work toward his concept of 'the aggregation of marginal gains.' Applying Brailsford's revolutionary concept to the British cyclist sport has resulted in its rise to world prominence. The concept is simple: isolate every factor that contributes to success or failure, and then do each one a little better. From riders having their own beds and pillows brought to the race location so that they can get a slightly better night's rest than the other riders, to diet, training, ergonomics, and technical improvements in their equipment, Brailsford contends there is no factor too small to ignore. These marginal gains, when taken together, combine into a radical aggregate change. Each improvement in discipline or training is small when taken in isolation, but the total change to the ultimate outcome is undeniable.

It is hard but thrilling to imagine what kind of change would be possible through the marginal gains of love applied to all of our lives, and not only our own lives but the contexts in which we live. Jesus gives us the command to love not because it is weak and sentimental but because it constitutes the overthrow of this world's corrupt systems. It is a power play.

When we meet an addict, do they need a friend? Warmth? A hug? Perhaps, but do they not also need power? Power to overcome? Power to learn? Power to work? When you hear of a house full of girls being trafficked from one country to another for sex slavery, do they just need sentimental love? A kind word? Sympathy? Don't they really need power? Power to escape? Power to fight off their oppressor? Power to rebuild their lives? Wasn't it the imbalance of power that kept them at the mercy of an oppressor in the first place?

Show me power without love, and I will show you the worst of humans. We all have experienced it: abuse, misconduct, harassment, oppression, stealing, betrayal, violence. These all expose the raw potential of the exercise of power without love.

The abuser is clearly not a godly model for leadership (power without love), but what of the enabling parent or friend of the abuser who denied or justified their violent and selfish behavior for years (love without power) in the name of love? That is no less a failed model for leadership in our families, businesses, and the church.

Everything that Jesus calls us to as leaders is an exercise of love and power. Justice: Love for the oppressed. Power to be free. Evangelism: Love for the lost. Power to be forgiven. Teaching: Love for the confused. Power to understand. Service: Love for those in need. Power to meet that need.

All of the world's great revolutionary leaders have taught us that to opt out of the struggle for power in the world (in the name of love or anything else) is to side with those who already have the power. It is to vote for the status quo.

We have wrestled with why the church has often done so poorly with power. Theologically, this is vexing since we should be the ones to wield it best. Our conclusion: first, we have not understood the full dimension of the call to love. Second, we have not acknowledged that we are also brokers of power and not just of love.

Why are church splits and church drama so bad? So loveless? Why is the business community—and even the government—often better with power than the church? It's because they expect it, and we are unfamiliar with it. It's because we are not acknowledging that we have it, and that it is a part of our inheritance and therefore a part of our responsibility. We are not accountable for what we claim we do not have.

When Jesus stood outside the tomb of Lazarus, weeping with his friend's sister, he prayed a public prayer. "I thank you that you hear me." The text gives us a window into his emotional state as well. What gets translated as "deeply moved and troubled" could easily be rendered "moved in anger." Jesus was upset. A careful reading of the text does not make plain exactly who or what is the object of his rage. Certainly not Mary or Martha, not the disciples, not the crowds. Perhaps he is angry at death itself. I imagine his lips pressed together in angry determination as he says, "take away the stone." Love must destroy what is against love. Jesus was born not just to die, but to live, though he die. "Did I not tell you that if you believe you would see the glory of God?" "I am the resurrection..." It is a story of a love that is stronger than death. It is the story of a tender and angry, weeping Jesus who is comfortable with his power.

We should be too. Jesus understood his own authority, knowing how to use it, and what guided it. Because of that, his love was not impotent; it was strong and capable, always wielded in the service of others. We do not have a record of Jesus performing a miracle for himself. Imagine the temptation. This is our model for selfless exercise of power. We retain power only long enough to give it away, or to use it in the service of others.

The call to love is not a call to sentimentality. It is a call to lead, and in so doing to change the world. Jesus knows what he is doing, and what he is releasing on the world. The marginal gains of a loving church could have a devastatingly beautiful effect on this world at war with evil.

It all sounds good, so why don't we love like Jesus? We don't because we protect ourselves. Love is dangerous. Love is loss. Love is sacrifice. Love is exposure and vulnerability. It is an act of defiance against selfishness and self-preservation. Love is knowing that you have power and then sharing it.

LOVE AS EMPOWERMENT

For the last 30 years, the seminal leadership concept in both secular and sacred leadership literature has been 'vision.' Seen as the holy grail of leadership theory, the key to visionary leadership seems to always be communication. Theorist like John Kotter have argued that you cannot under communicate vision, take whatever you are doing and multiply it 1,000 times.[9] This overstatement is meant to echo the almost religious fervor with which leaders have laid claim to a notion that was once relegated to the realm of fairy tales and theophany. Prophets and Seers have visions, and those who listen and follow, who would be adherents, must also be believers. The listener has to believe that the dream or vision was given to the seer as divine gift. We find the use of this language in an a-religious leadership world very telling. The implication is that a leader's followers (whether they believe in a God or not) must attribute godlike gifts to the leader they follow. They must believe that the vision of the future they have seen is both desirable and possible. The leader then must "cast" this vision to their audience, presumably in order to awaken the loyalty, and labor of the listener.

The problem with this notion of visionary leadership in the church is not that we can't believe in the prophetic, we *do,* it is that this kind of leadership requires the corresponding demand of alignment. In the church, the bearer of the vision is claiming more than just a good idea or a possible direction to go in, they are offering God's actual plan. This means that all those who would walk under that leader are asked to "get on board" with the vision of the church. Practically then, this too often means restricting the work and investment of the people in the church to the programs of the church, and nothing else.

Leaders who have taken this mandate to be a visionary leader to heart have fallen victim to an unbiblical view of leadership. Where is this concept in the bible? "Without vision the people perish?"[10] One verse?

These leaders see themselves cast in the Old Testament archetype of Moses. They are God's singular leader, the consolidation of his friendship, and will to lead a deaf and rebellious people. Moses goes up the mountain (that none of the common people can even touch or they will die), and talks to the God that is beyond their reach. When he comes down from the mountain of prayer, he is embedded with both the glory and the words of God. He is glowing, for goodness' sake. This archetype is consistent with the image of a visionary leader. They comprehend and then deliver the vision, and the rest of us need only follow it. Their work is receiving the vision, and our work is aligning to it.

But is this appropriate for the church? What about the priesthood of all believers? The cross has forever changed the dynamics of a leader's relationship with their people. First, as we have argued, their leadership must be governed by servanthood.

The visionary leader would make every person a servant to their vision, yet the church already has a leader: Jesus. He is the head of the church. He is the firstborn from among the dead. He is the first and the last. He is the author and the perfecter of our faith. He is the head of his church. Not us.

Our work as under-shepherds and servant leaders then is not to tell people what the vision of God is for them, but to show them the way up the mountain. It is not to be Moses for them, but to show them that because of Jesus we can all have the kind of intimate friendship with God that Moses enjoyed. We are the first to go, and the first to teach others where to go. The rabbis tell us that the Torah (Law) was given on a very specific day: the feast of Shavuot. That might not register until we call it by its more familiar New Testament name, the day of Pentecost. God provided his Spirit on the anniversary of the day he provided his Law. The Spirit was poured out—not upon one believer—but upon *all* believers. We all drink of the same Spirit. "Your young men will see visions, your old men will dream dreams."[11]

In the Old Testament revelation, leadership was often consolidated in one person. In the New Testament, leadership is shared. Ephesians 4 gives us a picture of the church growing into its full maturity under the leadership of five different kinds of leaders, each with a different kind of identifiable gift or affinity.

The vision school would say that "vision leaks" and that it must, for that reason, be constantly shared. The vision of a church, like the vision of a corporation, must be etched in glass in the lobby, printed on all the literature, and burned onto the hearts of the people—but let's ask why? It's because we keep forgetting. If we cannot remember the vision of the church, isn't that evidence that it is not actually in our hearts?

Simply put, we object to this kind of leadership in its conception and application. It has created corporate churches that overstate the place and influence of the primary leader, and in so doing block the creativity and apostolic impulse of its people. This is an area that the church has *not* been different. We have withheld and hoarded power that actually is not ours, and rightly belongs to God's people.

Besides that, we have lost the biblical concept of vision. That word was ours before it was a business concept, and it should still be in use by our prophets and our dreamers. Vision is our word because we all need supernatural sight of God, his kingdom, and the future he imagines for us. It is a religious word, and it should be the purview of the church, but it has been co-opted by the business world and then sold back to us twisted and vacant of its true meaning. Visions should be offered (like all prophecy) as edification of the people, not as a measured alignment of allegiance. We love our people, and for that reason, we release them to listen to God and follow his vision for their lives.

The church should not be a place where one visionary leader acts as the single mediator between the common people and God. The church should be a place where everyone has visions and dreams. The responsibility of ecclesial leadership is to create environments where dreams and visions are common place and, even more to the point, where people who get a vision from God can actually pursue it without being ostracized as someone who is not "on board with the Pastor's vision."

LOVE AS PERMISSION

The etymology of the word 'permission' is difficult to discern with certainty. The obvious derivative is the Latin root for 'mission.' Permission is certainly connected to mission. The 'per' could mean 'before' or, as I am more drawn to, somehow connected to the root 'father.' If it is, then consider the implications and the significance of that word in the work of Christian leadership.

Permission, then, is the father of mission. This means that mission will not happen without permission, and in the rare cases when it does, it is orphaned. We speak for so many disempowered entrepreneurs in the church when we say this is the case. Too many of us have had to go rogue and operate outside the blessing of our local churches in order to follow what we sense is the leadership and calling of God in our lives, and we have heard the same story over and over, a meeting that goes something like this:

Young leader: "I had an idea to reach out to *(insert mission idea here)* so I went to my pastor about it."

Mike or Brian: (wincing) "How did that go?"

Young leader: "He told me that it was not the direction the church was going. Not in line with the vision of the church."

Mike or Brian: "So he said no?"

Young leader: "Pretty much, he said if I do it the church will not be supporting it."

Really? We think that spiritual leadership that best represents Jesus would say no? Our answer to anyone who claims to have heard God call them to something is always "Yes." The real work of the church has to be helping that young disciple lead well, thrive, and not stumble. The church should be incubators for the entrepreneurial impulse in the hearts of our people. Not only are most churches lousy at helping this kind of initiative, they often actually forbid it. How dare we? How can we claim to be providing leadership for the church—the most empowered, creative, leadership-affirming body in history—if we say no to people who sense God nudging them to serve others? The power of the gospel is that anyone, from any people, class, or place, can become a servant leader in the church. Apostles, prophets, evangelists, teachers, and shepherds are not members of an elite *class.* They are called and equipped by an elite *God,* who stands alone in his sufficiency and can therefore call and gift whomever he pleases. There is a correlation between our reverence for God's ability to empower, and the breadth of our leadership's empowerment.

We are not saying that every idea we hear is actually from God. People want to start things for a million horrible reasons. We aren't saying that we should not be discerning in the conversation, asking them to think about what they are proposing or to count the cost of embarking on the journey—but it is akin to someone coming to us and asking if they can pray to put their faith in Jesus. Do you ever say no to that? We might ask for more information.

We might even think they might not totally mean it, discerning some hidden motivation, but both humility and hope demand that we still lead them in that prayer, because the desire is sacred.

In the same way, when someone comes to us wanting to engage the world around them with the good news, we have to stand in reverent awe of Jesus at work in one of his students, inviting them into the life of selflessness and mission.

LOVE AS COMMISSION (THE SHARING OF MISSIONAL AUTHORITY AND POWER)

In the final act of the discipleship narrative in Matthew, Jesus meets his students one last time on the mountainside where he once taught them to love their enemies and turn the other cheek:

> Then the eleven disciples went to Galilee, to the mountain where Jesus had told them to go. When they saw him, they worshiped him; but some doubted. Then Jesus came to them and said, "All authority in heaven and on earth has been given to me. Therefore go and make disciples of all nations, baptizing them in the name of the Father and of the Son and of the Holy Spirit, and teaching them to obey everything I have commanded you. And surely I am with you always, to the very end of the age."[12]

His moral teaching had an authority that was undeniable, as if he were not just talking about something he had discovered about morality, but as if he was its original author. Yet, the narrative is made opaque by what scholars call the messianic secret. In his journey toward the cross, he tries to hide his true messianic identity, often telling his followers to keep the news of his miraculous power a secret. That is, until he is resurrected. After that final gesture of supernatural power and ultimate authority he meets his disciples on the same mountain, and they worship him. Gone is the messianic secret, and gone in the prohibition from Jesus "not to tell anyone."[13] For the first time, he accepts worship and unveils the full weight of his true identity.

"All authority, in heaven and earth, has been given to me."[14] We know the rest. North American evangelicals pride themselves on knowing the rest. We define ourselves by branding this as the Great Commission, and then commit its pieces to memory. "Go and make disciples" is the evangelical manifesto, and yet there is a meta-message here that we do not often see.

Immediately after claiming total authority in heaven and on earth, he empowers his students. If there ever was a leader that should micromanage, that should "just do it himself," that deserved to be alone at the top of a bottomless hierarchy, it was the resurrected Jesus. Yet, he empowers them. It is as if he is saying, you know I have all authority, not you, so here is my authority. Jesus makes one final gesture of love. He gives them power.

This is not just an ecclesiological reality. It is an eschatological one as well. In the Revelation of John, there is a breathtaking scene of the throne room of God; a place that before this was only seen in the prophet's dreams. Neither Daniel nor Ezekiel has such a clear rendition of the beginning of the end and the architecture of heavens ruling center:

> At once I was in the Spirit, and there before me was a throne in heaven with someone sitting on it. And the one who sat there had the appearance of jasper and ruby. A rainbow that shone like an emerald encircled the throne. Surrounding the throne were twenty-four other thrones, and seated on them were twenty-four elders. They were dressed in white and had crowns of gold on their heads.[15]

The throne of God is appropriately placed, as in Daniel's vision, in the middle of the worshipping throng numbering in the thousands—but what is a new revelation in John's vision (and one we have yet to discover) is that there are 24 *other* thrones surrounding him. This bends the mind. When the world is finally put right and the veil of human sin and unbelief has been lifted, when all that is wrong is judged and made right, when the rightful ruler of this world comes to take his rightful place on the throne of this world, there will be 24 other thrones present? Why? Because God always shares power with his people. Not just in this age, when he needs his mission accomplished by his church, but in the age to come, when he rules and reigns unabated. He has made us to be a kingdom of priests to serve our God and King.

Now, in this final scene, those thrones *do* sit empty as those assigned to them bow in front of them instead of sitting in his presence. They do not wear the crowns that he has won for them, instead throwing them at his feet because they know that their leadership in his presence has a kind of *absurdity* to it—but those thrones and crowns exist with his permission and will. Staggeringly, in the perfection of time, God will still be looking to share his rule and his authority with us. This is important in ways I am sure I do not understand, but one necessary application has to be the sharing of power in our own leadership. Simply put, if the resurrected Jesus—the perfect judge of humankind—can share power, how do we explain why we don't? If Jesus can share his authority with imperfect human beings of limited understanding and wavering obedience (which includes you and me), then why can't we? When we hold authority, we are mirrors of this world and not the one to come. We are indifferent toward Jesus and his call to another kind of leadership.

> You know that the rulers of the Gentiles lord it over them, and their high officials exercise authority over them. Not so with you.[16]

What kind of leaders must we be? We must be the kind of leaders that serve the missionary impulse placed inside our people by God, even refusing to ask them to do anything for us that might distract them or delay them in following that sense of calling. We must be fathers and mothers, supervisors and teachers, leaders and friends who freely have received, and therefore freely give, both love and power.

ONE
TWO
THREE
FOUR
FIVE
SIX
SEVEN

EIGHT

NINE
TEN
ELEVEN
TWELVE

Embodiment and a Faith that Saves

Your life is a sermon and you are always preaching it.

Some time ago, I was talking with a friendly stranger when the conversation became increasingly personal and spiritual. As I began to introduce what I thought would be a clever presentation of the gospel, I could see that she was emotionally checking out. Her eyes rolled. Her body language changed. She was clearly agitated. "What's wrong?" I asked. "Let me tell you my name," she suggested. It sounded remotely familiar. Then she dropped the bomb. "I am the illegitimate daughter of a very successful pastor. He gives me monthly support to stay out of his business and out of his way. Forgive the disrespect, but the last thing I need is another sermon. His life is preaching loud and clear."

That's the point. Your life is your sermon, and you're preaching it everyday. This is where Christians tend to blow it. They serve up some really biblical truth in some really nauseating ways. They major on minors and minor on majors. They tend to be extremely unaware of the disconnect between their supposed faith and their actual lives, but hypocrisy is like bad breath— everybody knows you have it except for you. If you've ever spent time with non-Christians you know that the first step is almost always apologizing for the hypocrisy of Christians.

DISEMBODIED FAITH

If we're honest, hypocrisy is not just a religious problem; it's a human problem. We hear conservatives raising their voice about

117

homosexuality, and their catch phrase is often family values. Imagine how much it will mess up a kid who is being raised by two women, the reasoning goes. A child needs a mother and a father, they say. Yet those with opposing views may wonder how conservatives can talk about family values when more than 50% of them get divorced. They see a community of people that do *not* stay married trying to talk about marital morality. How ironic.

On the other hand, we hear liberals raising their voice in the name of social justice and helping the needy. Yet when the numbers are crunched we find a troubling trend: while political liberals claim to possess a concern for the needs of others, they personally sacrifice considerably less of their income than their conservative counterparts.[1] In other words, when the rubber meets the road, they're not as compassionate as their political positions boast. People are very motivated to fight injustice—unless of course it costs them something personally.

Hypocrisy is the human status quo, which is why the church must be different. We are the only message most people will ever hear, and few things irritate like a mixed message. We're already preaching; so the question is: what message do we embody?

The essence of the kingdom of Jesus cannot be reduced to the printed page of a gospel tract; it's supposed to come with skin. The apostle Paul did not simply write epistles on paper; he wrote his message on flesh. "Clearly you are an epistle of Christ, ministered by us, written not with ink but by the Spirit of the living God, not on tablets of stone but on tablets of flesh, that is, of the heart."[2] The gospel must be proclaimed, but it comes alive when embodied. Few books nail this truth like the book of James. "What good is it, my brothers, if someone says he has faith but does not have works? Can that faith save him? So faith by itself, if it does not have works, is dead."[3]

What a great question: "Can that faith save him?" James knows exactly what he's doing as he writes these words. It's not like James disregards faith; he talks about it all the time: the testing of our faith,[4] asking in faith,[5] holding faith,[6] the prayer of faith.[7] He knows Jesus' promise of eternal life to whosoever believes in him.[8] The issue is not grace versus law or the presence of faith versus absence of faith. The question is, are we dealing with *saving* faith or *that* faith? There is a living faith, and then there is a dead faith. It's a soteriological question: can a non-embodied faith save you?

EMBODIED FAITH

Consider the typical Christian approach to salvation and the assurance thereof. "'Abraham believed God, and it was counted to him as righteousness.' And he was called the friend of God."[9] We lean on the story of Abraham as one of the great proof texts for salvation by faith. Yet what was it that Abraham believed when God accounted it to him as righteousness? It was not that Abraham would have a cosmic change of spiritual status that purchased his position in heaven when he died. We read the account in Genesis 15. God told this childless man that his descendants would be like the stars of heaven, and Abraham took God at his word. What follows is not the story of an infallible man with a flawless faith, but a righteous man with an embodied faith.

We tell people they are justified before God because they believe in the death of Jesus—but what about the life of Jesus? What about the resurrection of Jesus? Far too much of our gospel presentation fails to touch the real life, in the real world, in a real way. To be sure, the death of Jesus delivers us from the death penalty of sin, but there is more to salvation than a pardon. Once you get out of jail, you still need to live. There is more to redemption than freedom from the consequences of our sin; Jesus promised freedom from sin itself. This could not be more practical. Once you're declared not-guilty, you need to know what to do with your freedom.

Let's be honest, the way most gospel presentations go, all we needed was a substitutionary death. Yet the New Testament is obsessed with a gospel that goes all the way to a resurrection. Why? Because we need a salvation that brings more than justification; we need a salvation of *regeneration*. We need a gospel that resurrects us to new life, not just the reassurance of a new heaven.

> But someone will say, 'You have faith and I have works.' Show me your faith apart from your works, and I will show you my faith by my works.[10]

According to James, true justification always leads to regeneration. True faith always leads to action. We already know what you believe; your life is preaching loud and clear.

I (Mike) remember the day one of my sons lovingly assured his grandmother that when he grew up he would take care of her. He was so young and his words were so kind that my mother-in-law was obviously touched. It was a special moment—but it would not last long. "If you really mean it," she responded, "you'll need to go to college and get a good job, which means you need to do your homework." I'll never forget his immediate response: "Never mind."

Talk is cheap. My son was saying that if his commitment demanded some sort of an intersection with the real world, then he'd need to reconsider. James is saying that saving faith always leads to a gracious collision with the real world.

> You believe that there is one God. You do well. Even the demons believe – and tremble![11]

People say, "I have faith." Perhaps, but it may be like the faith of a demon. It's *that* faith, not saving faith. It's faith in theory, not faith through resurrection.

> But do you want to know, O foolish man, that faith without works is dead?[12]

We sometimes get the privilege of engaging in interfaith dialogue with university students from various cultures. Our message always finds its way back to the sheer power of the resurrection of Jesus. It's a stunning truth that demands a verdict. And yet, these encounters are regularly sidetracked when the conversation shifts from the deeds of Jesus to the deeds of Christians. Why don't Christians look more like Jesus? How do we explain the Crusades? How do we explain so much greed? How do we explain the lack of distinction in sexual purity between believers and non-believers? To which some well-meaning believer usually drops the infamous but worthless cliché: We Christians aren't perfect. We're just forgiven. In other words, we don't look more like Jesus because all he gave us was forgiveness.

James calls such a line of thinking a dead theology from a dead faith. Faith alone saves, but the faith that saves is never alone. It starts like a seed, but this seed is so potent that it grows into something which infiltrates every aspect of our lives.

We read about this reality in the lives of the early Christians in the book of Acts. Their faith was not flawless, but it was absolutely embodied and the watching world could not help but pay attention. Saving faith changed everything as the sick were healed, the lawless became pure, the materialistic became generous, and entire cities were transformed. Acts 2 ends with these words: "...praising God and having favor with all the people. And the Lord added to the church daily those who were being saved."[13] The gospel alone is the power of God for salvation, but it is usually never heeded until it is first embodied.

Tony Campolo makes the point with a story of a Marxist student leader he met while doing work in the Dominican Republic. Campolo had connected with a Christian doctor named Elias Santana who had sacrificed a potentially lucrative medical practice in America to go back to his homeland and give himself to his people, working among the poorest of the poor. Whatever profits he made from his practice, he would spend to buy medicine for the impoverished in the slums of the city.

One day they drove into one of the most dangerous sections of Santo Domingo to set up shop and provide medical care for those in need. After laboring all day, Elias honked his horn, got up on his truck, and began to present the gospel of Jesus. While listening to the makeshift sermon, Tony noticed this very outspoken Marxist leader, Pedro. Tony approached him and commented that Pedro had better watch out or Elias would get all these people to follow Jesus; then there wouldn't be anybody left to follow Pedro. "What am I supposed to say?" he replied. Then he pointed to the preacher and said, "Elias Santana has earned the right to be heard."

That's the point: Our deeds do not earn our salvation, but they certainly earn our right to be heard. This is why James says, "Show me your faith..." It's not a call to lower the volume of our proclamation of the gospel of Jesus. It's an appeal to once again allow the Word to take on flesh and dwell among us.

As communicators one of our temptations is to labor to string together ideas that produce memorable material. Yet the longer we serve the more we see that people don't need life-changing messages nearly as much as they need to see lives that have been changed by the message.

THE FRUIT OF ACTION

There is a reason that this second chapter of James has been a thorn in the side to untold numbers of so-called faith-only Christians ever since the Reformation. Scripture is clear that we are saved by grace through faith, "...not of works, lest anyone should boast."[15]

> Was not Abraham our father justified by works when he offered Isaac his son on the altar?[14]

But James forces the "believer" to be brutally honest about the nature of their belief. Is it a saving faith, or a hollow faith? Abraham was made righteous in Genesis 15 when he believed God, but he was *proved* righteous in Genesis 22 when he offered his son. The root is faith. The fruit is action.

Martin Luther King, Jr. preached a faith in non-violence all across the country. But on September 28, 1962, he *proved* it when a member of the American Nazi Party vaulted onto a stage, interrupted his sermon, and proceeded to beat him mercilessly.

When King finally made his way to his feet, the word became flesh. He instinctively dropped his arms and refused to retaliate. "Don't touch him," he would instruct the crowd of civil rights leaders. "We have to pray for him." That message was *in* him. His life was his message.

We've almost come to expect disappointment. Politicians, parents, teachers, and spiritual leaders alike all let us down. It's actually easier to brace oneself for the hypocrisy. We know that people are far greater on the outside than the inside, and we accept that we live in a society of image-maintenance and a culture of the bottom line. As long as a leader possesses a gift, generates a good economy, and produces a good speech, we comply. Frankly, it's a surprise to find leaders who live the message they claim.

In an age of unprecedented cynicism few things provide more missional mileage than an individual who surprises us with integrity. If you are a leader, we hope you hear the call to be different. Leadership instruction specializes in teaching us to produce, but what if your life is not worth following? You need to get a life.

> Beloved, I beg you as sojourners and pilgrims, abstain from fleshly lusts which war against the soul, having your conduct honorable among the Gentiles, that when they speak against you as evildoers, they may, by your good works which they observe, glorify God in the day of visitation.[16]

I remember reading the story of a missionary of a past century who discovered that the "natives" he was trying to reach with his words had been distracted by his actions. Every night they would peek into his hut. Every morning they would follow him to the river. Every day they would observe his activities and mannerisms—and they were offended by his lifestyle. One of the reasons the "natives" in our lives are not listening is because they're watching.

Many a skeptic has studied the life and ministry of Mother Teresa with the goal of finding something to mar her character.

Yet she is a great white hole for the atheist in us. While much has been written to disagree with her beliefs, it is hard to deny her fruit. Her life was her sermon.

We are already preaching; so what's the message? Somehow, our movements must embrace a radical commitment to fully embody the faith we embrace. We are in desperate need of leaders committed to both orthodoxy (right doctrine) and orthopraxy (right living). This chapter is a call to live lives worth following. We need leaders who actually have a life. We need truly living epistles.

Our deeds are not the source of our salvation, but they are the *course* of our salvation. Sometimes this calls for the deeds of engagement, while at other times it demands deeds of abstinence. You can answer the question with your own principles. Do you claim to believe you should not commit adultery? Then don't look at a woman lustfully because "whoever looks at a woman to lust for her has already committed adultery with her in his heart."[17] Dump porn, and eliminate compromising situations. "If your right eye causes you to sin, pluck it out and cast it from you."[18] Get so serious about lust that you'd rather cancel your internet connection than continue to live in hypocrisy.

Do you claim to believe in love? Then share. "But whoever has this world's goods, and sees his brother in need, and shuts up his heart from him, how does the love of God abide in him?"[19] Don't wait for a sign. Don't wait to be asked. When you see a need, respond.

Do you claim to believe in the mercy of God? Then show mercy when people harm you, insult you, and forget you. "Bear with one another, and forgive one another, if anyone has a complaint against another; even as Christ forgave you, so you also must do."[20]

Do you claim to believe in a gospel that says we are accepted by a holy God? Then, "Do not hold the faith of our Lord Jesus Christ, the Lord of glory, with partiality."[21] Pay attention to the stranger. Make space for the awkward. Create space for the outcast.

Do you claim to believe in justice? Then "Open your mouth for the speechless... judge righteously, and plead the cause of the poor and needy."[22] Do what you can where you can. Speak up when you see a bully. Make your spending patterns increasingly ethical. Support ministries that rescue children from slavery. Realize that the justice most needed is almost always unpopular. Stand for justice before it's popular and leverage your influence to make change even when it's not culturally acceptable or trendy.

Do you claim to believe that sin is defiling? Then get ruthless with your sin. "Confess your sins to one another, and pray for one another, that you may be healed."[23]

Do you believe in prayer? Then set your alarm and make time for it. Do you believe God has chosen to reveal himself through the Bible? Read it, study it, and memorize it. Do you believe God will supply all your needs? Then give first, spend second. Do you believe there is power of life and death in the tongue? Then keep your tongue from evil and your lips from speaking deceit. Do you believe Jesus is the truth? Then commit yourself to speaking the highest level of truth. Do you believe that Jesus is good news? Then open your mouth and share his message. Do you believe in the Word become flesh? Then put skin on your faith and live it. Otherwise, call it what it is: a disembodied faith.

Hypocrisy: everybody hates it, and yet everybody expects it, which makes the difference all the more meaningful. Imagine what would happen if our people did what they say they believe. Imagine if we lived lives where our families are the most impressed, our closest friends are the most convinced, and our fruit becomes the great white hole for the cynic in people. Trees are known by their fruit.

THE SOURCE OF EMBODIED FAITH

Here's the thing: The problem is never the *fruit*, it's always about the *root*. Different people are courageous enough to examine the fruit of their deeds, but they are also wise enough to focus on the root of their faith. Because life eventually flows from the inside out. Hypocrites guard their appearances, but the holy guard their hearts.

So what's going on in your heart? What deeds does your boredom pull out of you? What fruit do your trials squeeze out of you? Anger? Greed? Withdrawal? Fear? Selfishness? Shame? Why do we feel this way? Why do we talk this way? Why do we turn to comfort food? Why do we overwork?

When people ask us, "Why can't I forgive myself," that's bad fruit. Yet the real issue is a root. Although we may claim to believe in a Savior of mercy and grace, our true faith is in something else. A pseudo-savior, an alternate faith in an alternate god. It's an idol, and idols do not forgive.

James raises the pivotal question. Can an alternate faith—a false god—save you? Of course not. So renounce false faith and dead gods and obtain a true faith in the living God. Obtain the faith that really saves.

This is not simply a call to walk the walk, every good leadership book makes that point. This is more than a call to clarify your convictions so that you will live a truly authentic life, although yes, we are saying that, too. This is a call to get the right faith: a saving faith, which is why the secret will never be trying harder, but instead trusting more deeply in the One who lived this in spades.

He claimed to care for his creation. He claimed to love his people, but he did more than talk. He knew we'd never fully live up to our faith claims because we have a chronic heart problem. Hypocrisy runs in our family; it's been the status quo ever since the first Adam. So the second Adam did what the first Adam could not.

The Word became flesh and dwelt among us.[24] Mysteriously, gloriously, the pre-existent Son of God took on a body and showed us what it means to be truly human. Everything he asks us to do, he did. He walked in love. He wept with those who wept.

He rejoiced with those who rejoiced. He turned the other cheek. Ultimately, he was lifted up on an execution stake where he blessed those who cursed him and forgave those who wronged him. He fully lived the life we should have lived, and then he fully died the death we should have died. Then he rose from the dead in a glorified—but fully human—*body*. At the center of the gospel, as at the center of the story of your life, is embodiment.

ONE
TWO
THREE
FOUR
FIVE
SIX
SEVEN
EIGHT
NINE
TEN
ELEVEN
TWELVE

Widows and the Heresy of Half

Giving, like the rest of our life with God is done best when it comes from the heart. The prime example of giving in the New Testament is a woman who gave ALL she had. Beyond our money or resources the real call in giving is to give ourselves.

No matter what is wrong with the church, its structures, or its leaders, at the beating heart is always the people. We can reform and redeem the church because we are the church. We can alter any characteristic because it is ours to shape and love as an extension of our own lives. Complaining about what is wrong with the church is folly since it is ours to change. We should lay prophetic eyes upon the church so that we might live differently, and in so doing make her more beautiful.

If the Western church is selling out to consumerism and idolatry then we (each of us) should rekindle the fire of simplicity and devotion in our own hearts. The solution is there, in the reality of our own lives. Change is ours for the taking. And it starts with total surrender.

As long as we hold back some of our lives, some of our talent, some of our time, or some of our money, we undermine the kingdom of God, which rightly demands all that we have and are.

The widow in Mark 12 becomes our model for revolutionary change. Her story is preceded by an exposé on the alternative religious impulse of those who would follow God for show.

As he taught, Jesus said, "Watch out for the teachers of the law. They like to walk around in flowing robes and be greeted with respect in the marketplaces, and have the most important seats in the synagogues and the places of honor at banquets. They devour widows' houses and for a show make lengthy prayers. These men will be punished most severely."[1]

Jesus sat down opposite the place where offerings were given and watched the crowd putting their money into the temple treasury. Many rich people threw in large amounts, but a poor widow came and put in two very small copper coins, worth only a few cents.[2]

Calling his disciples to him, Jesus said, "Truly I tell you, this poor widow has put more into the treasury than all the others. They all gave out of their wealth; but she, out of her poverty, put in everything—all she had to live on."[3]

Jesus sits outside the temple, the place of religious expression, looking for illustrations of two very different ways of relating to God. One is to exploit and profit, and the other is to surrender and sacrifice.

THOSE WHO DEVOUR

There is a version of Christianity offered to our world that invites the adherent to devour. It sets up God as a kind of cosmic genie waiting to give you three wishes. More egregious manifestations of this thinking, heralding the prosperity of the faithful, have given way in recent years to a subtler, but equally devilish, version which implies that God mostly exists to make your life better. They reason that the more of God you have, the more successful and happy you will be. In the 1st century temple system (which Jesus is critiquing here) it was the common practice of the Scribes to take administrative control over the household of a widow. If no man was in place to take control of the woman's financial affairs, they would seize control (presumably for her own good) since she could not own or manage the property herself. They would take some—or all—of that wealth for themselves.

This was deeply troubling to Jesus, and part of the reason why it is the only place on earth we ever see him openly violent.

Presumably his own convictions come from God's design specifications for the temple, namely that it should exist to support and serve widows and orphans. They are meant to be the ones who receive from the temple offering. Instead of that offering being taken in order to help this widow, they allow her to give all she has, and give her nothing in return. They devour her. This is obviously reprehensible. Jesus certainly makes it clear that there will be a reckoning for their abuse and usury.

On the outside the story is about them, but on the inside it is about the woman who seems unaware of the injustice and comes to give all she has to God. On the outside, this is a condemnation of the Scribes, their false religion of the capital and the commerce of God. We are so quick to make this passage a sentimental tale about only the heart because we don't want to face the truth.

On the outside, this is about a widow being exploited by a bad religious system, with its false religion of the capitalization and commerce of God. It's about a poor widow who has the last of her money taken by corrupt leaders. Her household is devoured by the offering she gives.

On the outside, it is about the contrast between the scribes and the woman. They walk around in flowing robes while she is dressed so poorly that Jesus can tell she is a widow. They are greeted with respect in the marketplace (the place of commerce, where people make money) while she is ignored because she has nothing to buy or sell.

They have the most important seats in the worship service while she is excluded from worship, outside even the court of women. They sit at the places of honor at the banquets while she does not even have food to feed her children. On the outside, Jesus is condemning an offering system that was meant to take care of widows and orphans not bankrupt them. On the outside, this passage is about judgment.

But on the inside, at the center, is a woman who is seemingly unimportant and uninvolved. A woman who does not understand the folly and the Machiavellian games of these men. A woman who does not notice or comment on their sin or their error. She is not concerned with that. She is alone and in poverty and all she knows is that she needs God.

I (Brian) have had a lot to say over the years about the church and its misuse of money. For me, it is not just her sacrifice of money that is exemplary; it is her sacrifice of complaint. She does not want to tear the system down. She does not come in protest or anger. She certainly has the *right* to come that way, but what if she is a model to us not only in the surrendering of her money but in the need to be right while others are wrong. She is generous in ways we can barely understand. She does not come to change or challenge the system directly, she comes in desperate search for God. She offers him all that she has, and in so doing levels the most devastating critique possible. Her life, hunger, and pure heart are the best critiques of all. She has so little. She is faced with a choice in her mind; she does not trust that she can survive on these two coins. So she chooses to put her trust in God. This passage is about judgment, but perhaps not in the way we would expect.

JESUS IS WATCHING THE OFFERING

It is chilling to imagine Jesus sitting down as the judge of all the earth to preside over our places of our sacrifice and offering. I think that Jesus has chosen this location so that he can wait for just such a moment. I think he is sitting in judgment of this false system, the commerce of the temple, and waiting for an example of the people exploited by the system: the person devoured by the Scribes.

Yet when he sees her and actually watches spiritual exploitation happen, it seems like his focus changes. I think he is taken with her. He waits for an example of exploitation, but when he sees this widow he finds something more important than that problem. Her poverty of spirit and purity of heart eclipses their sin.

He does not say, "See, that is what I am talking about— exploitation! That woman just gave the last she has to line the pockets of these corrupt men!" Though that statement would have been true and a valid continuation of what he was teaching, he almost abandons that line of argument because he sees something more important, more *significant*. He sees something beautiful to God. He sees a woman surrendering the whole of her life.

It's not unlike a prosperity church that preys on the poor, or the late night television preacher who invites your widowed grandmother to give her last $100, only for it to line the pockets of some charlatan. That leader deserves their condemnation, but what of your grandmother? What she does, even though it is ill-conceived, is beautiful to God because it represents something more important than men and their money.

Jesus says the widow gives more because she gives out of her poverty, and that means that her gift is heroic and bathed in faith. Her gift is a cry for God. It is as if Jesus stops his critique to show his disciples something truly beautiful and right, and even this revelation flies in the face of our modern thoughts about giving. Practically, we think of giving out of abundance, the excess of overflow. We all wish we had more money so we could give more, because we want to pay our bills and *then* have enough left over to give. That view is not biblical. Religious leaders, on the other hand, tend to take an old covenant approach to giving. They ask us to give the first fruits or a tithe (money off the top).

What Jesus highlights here is neither the excess nor the first fruits; she gives ALL that she has to live on. Perhaps this is what Jesus was waiting to see: someone who would not play percentages with God, but who was so desperate that she would bet it all on him. The only gift worthy of God is *all*.

SHE GAVE ALL SHE HAD TO LIVE ON

When my (Brian) oldest daughter was in second grade, a boy asked her if she would be his girlfriend. As she tells the story, she had never heard of that and was therefore unsure about the terms of the request. She has always been a little entrepreneur, and perhaps sensing a business opportunity she asked him how much he was willing to pay. He offered 50 cents, and she accepted.

Once she got home she told me what happened. Incredulous, I told her, "Jael, you give that money back and you tell him, 'I am worth way more than 50 cents.'" She did, never to undervalue herself like that again.

It is almost farcical to think that my wildly bright and beautiful daughter could be bought for any amount of money—never mind so little—but this is an error we make in our relationship with God. What if that was all the money he had in the world? What if it were his life savings? Not just a lot of money to him, but *all* of his money? What if he pledged every dollar he would ever make in his lifetime to her in that schoolyard that day? That changes the offer because then it would not be about money, it would be about romance. *Some* is rude and cheap. It implies the recipient can be bought for a price. But *all* is romantic because it implies that you are worth everything. It says you are priceless.

When we hold back from God, we prove that we trust in those things more than him. We overestimate their place in our lives and underestimate his. And then we offer him *some*. How grotesque that we try to buy God off with a scandalous offering of half our lives, half our time, or half our future. How bizarre of us to imagine that God needs money, or for that matter *anything* from us. The only thing he wants is what he does not yet have: your heart. The parts of your life that remain under your control and not his are the only acceptable sacrifice for the God who has everything. When you think about it, the idea is both tender and liberating. He wants all of you.

We miss this truth sometimes because we have amassed so many things. Middle class people can be blinded by their abundance. The clarity of the widow must surely be related to her material poverty. She is poor enough to realize that what she has is not actually enough to live on. What she has amassed is not enough to sustain her. If you were down to your last $5 and it was all you had to live on for a week, you might find yourself sitting among your bills wondering what to do. Which child do I feed? Which bill do I pay? It is not enough, and here is the key: she recognizes that.

It's never enough, so she puts all her money on God. She has no Plan B, no contingency and no other hope. Now you begin to see why Jesus liked her so much. Jesus is not impressed with degrees or amounts. According to him, she has put in more because of her level of dependence. She gives more because she gives herself, her future, her hope for survival.

Ten years after the schoolyard boyfriend, Jael was being asked to the prom by one of her classmates. He was a lanky, gregarious whirlwind of a boy. She was *not* interested and said so, but he didn't give up. He started a marketing campaign to get Jael to go to prom with him. He asked her every day, trying various tactics including hand making posters with her life-sized face and plastering them all over school. The posters read "Jael, please come to prom with me."

This time my reaction was totally different. *She* may not have liked him, but I did. I started pulling for her to say yes to the kid. I couldn't convince her, but at least he understood that my daughter was worth an all out, full-scale campaign. Anything less would just not do. Here is the principle: it wins the heart of a father when his child is loved in such a way. Likewise, it moves our Father to see his son loved with abandon and without reservation.

What do you have to live on? Not just your money, but what do you have to trust in? Jesus wants it all. He might end up giving a lot of it back to you (he doesn't need it after all), but that is his call because it really should all be his anyway.

Still, I am convinced that the only way we will ever give him everything is if we can somehow come to the conclusion that what we have amassed, what we have made for ourselves is not enough. No matter how much we have it is woefully insufficient. It cannot save us, it cannot satisfy us, it cannot heal us, and it cannot make us whole. And so we give, but not the first or the last of what we have, but *all* that we have to live on.

GIVING UP A LIFE WITHOUT PAIN

His infinite worth must be met with the full surrender of our lives. We surrender first because he is worthy (and he commands it), and then because it is good for us. A life lived with God will be hard, but it will be worth it. A life surrendered to God will take you into the fray, and you will find pain there—but the notion that we can live a life without pain is an illusion anyway. The difference is that the surrendered life can find peace, holiness, and meaning in the midst of that pain. All of us suffer, but when God has your life your suffering can serve a greater purpose.

I was in the Philippines last year investing in some of our leaders there. Like so many of our international co-laborers, these Filipino leaders teach us about what a life of surrender and sacrifice really means. Their labor among the poorest of the earth is breathtakingly beautiful and also exhausting beyond our middle class comprehension. One night, I listened to one of our most dedicated leaders pour out her heart and pain. She was looking for answers as she had come to the end of her own resources.

"I just get so tired. I feel overwhelmed sometimes," she said. With tears streaming down her face she confessed, "I love them so much, Brian. I want to give myself to Jesus, even to my dying breath, but sometimes I just wear out."

What was my response? I will be honest, there is a psycho-selfish reflex in me that is in many of us. As Americans, we carry a kind of Freudian self-infatuation and take pride in our ingenuity. In other words, we are self-centered, and we think we can fix anything. I became uncomfortable with her discomfort. I searched my mind for the solution. It was partly compassion and partly self-interest. What is causing her pain, and how can I remove it?

Problem: Something is hurting you.

Solution: Get rid of it.

Think about that for a second. Your marriage is causing you pain? Then get out of it. Your job is wearing on you? Quit. Your schedule is too busy? Do less. Your calling is wearing you out? Cut back. Always this is our reflex—but then I remember whose we are and what we do. I remember the God who has called us, and the nature of that calling, and my response to her went something like this: "What did you think it was going to be like? To rescue slaves from the clutches of sin and death? To walk among the poor and tell them stories of the God who became poor? To lead the resistance against evil by whispering rumors of redemption?" I really looked at her, with admiration and love, and instead of trying to negate or remove the pain, the struggle, and the fight, I simply reminded her of something even more important. "God is pleased with you. You are a true daughter of the kingdom—and whatever it costs you it is worth it."

Sure, sometimes things are hard because we screw up, or because we are doing the wrong things, or doing the *right* things in the wrong way—but sometimes there is nothing to fix. Sometimes we are actually living the life of Christ in the world. Isn't it true that Jesus gave himself for us? That he became a sacrifice for us, giving all that he had to live on so that we might live and know God?

> This is the gospel that you heard and that has been pro-claimed to every creature under heaven, and of which I, Paul, have become a servant.[4]

> Now I rejoice in what I am suffering for you, and I fill up in my flesh what is still lacking in regard to Christ's afflictions...[5]

No servant is greater than his master. When you decided to give Jesus your life, when you said you would pay any price, did you not think he would accept your offering?

GOD RECIEVES THE OFFERING

Maybe we think we are going to be like Abraham and take our Isaac to the mountain and offer him to God, and God will say, "Psyche! I just wanted to see if you were willing." That is why corporate worship and singing is invalid if we are not also embodying the words of worship and surrender that we sing.

We want to sing, "Have it all Lord," and then have him not really keep it. Like we surrender our lives in the worship service but fully expect that he will be standing at the door when the service is over, handing it back to us as we leave. Here is the unspoken element to this story: They keep this widow's money. It is all she has to live, and Jesus doesn't say, "She needs it, give it back to her." He lets it stay in the treasury, because he knows that (in her heart) she has given it to God.

He measures it for what it is, all that she has, and therefore sees it as an acceptable sacrifice for God. Faith is what pleases God. However much you have, offer it to God. Putting the little faith we have in *him,* not our wealth, our robes, our respect, our positions, or our place in this world. Jesus showed, once and for all, what God wants.

The only thing that counts is faith expressing itself in love.[6] Jesus condemns the temple system and the people who have corrupted it—and then he dies for them.

ONE
TWO
THREE
FOUR
FIVE
SIX
SEVEN
EIGHT
NINE
TEN
ELEVEN
TWELVE

Sweet Tea and the Wind of God

*Too much of our experience has relegated the work and person
of the Holy Spirit to the sidelines of life and ministry. Yet, there
can be no life or breath in the lungs of our message without His
abiding work in and through us. We must remember and revive
the work and wind of the Holy Spirit.*

W hat a facinating question. *Did you receive the Spirit
when you believed?* These were the apostle Paul's
opening words upon meeting a group of disciples in
Ephesus. It's a *different* question. Think about the questions most
21ˢᵗ-century Christians ask when they meet a "disciple" for the
first time. What church do you go to? What authors do you read?
Are you reformed? Pre-trib? Complementarian? What's your
position on eternal security? Instead, there is this question from
the apostle. *Did you receive the Spirit?*

Do our people talk like that? We are betting that he knew
something we don't know. Why might Paul be asking a question
like this in Acts 19? Might we suggest it is because he had already
been marked by the history-altering experiment of the previous
18 chapters of the book? This was not theory or mere theology.
This was his experience. This was their experience, and we long
for it to be ours.

We continue to hear various Bible teachers go out of their
way to dissuade people from using the book of Acts as some kind
of an example of a golden age of the church worthy of emulation.
There are no true examples, the reasoning goes. There will not
be a golden age until Jesus returns and makes all things new, so

don't get distracted looking to any group—including the early church—as examples worthy of imitation. The argument has the ring of wisdom to it, but it simply does not stand up to the test of Scripture.

We cannot help but believe this is precisely why our sovereign God has ordained to preserve the book of Acts in the canon. It is a case study, perhaps even an invitation, if you have ears to hear. These 28 chapters are not a model of perfection, but they are absolutely a snapshot of people becoming "partakers of the divine nature, having escaped the corruption that is in the world."[1] They were very clearly fruitful, effective, and different. Why do we have the book of Acts? I believe for the purpose of Hebrews 6:12: "Do not be sluggish, but imitators of those who through faith and patience inherit promises."

Acts is supposed to make us hungry. It is supposed to stir our hearts to believe that God actually answers the prayer, *on earth as it is in heaven.* Let's go imitate our brothers and sisters who inherited promises, and there is no greater promise than "the promise of the Father."[2]

ACTS EXPERIMENT

In Acts 2, we read about the birth of the Church as God pours out his Spirit. When asked to explain this clearly overwhelming experience, the apostle Peter connected the event to Joel's prophecy about the last days: "And in the last days it shall be, God declares, that I will pour out my Spirit on all flesh."[3] You can't even explain the subversive and revolutionary nature of the earliest church without recognizing their perceived self-identity as an eschatological people. That is, they saw themselves to be the very participants of the strategic "last days." What was the sign of these last days? The outpouring of the Spirit.

The result of this first Spirit experience was stunning. A very typical gospel presentation produced 3000 baptisms, which jumpstarts a wave of boldness and power that produces the momentum that would turn the known world upside down. Yet the writer of Acts (Luke) consistently goes out of his way to connect the dots lest the reader miss this pivotal ingredient: "And when they had prayed... they were all *filled with the Holy Spirit* and continued to speak the word of God with boldness."[4] For the early believers boldness was not the forced reality of a group of striving religionists, it was the natural response to the experience of the Spirit. "You will receive power when the Holy Spirit comes upon you."[5]

In Acts 6, the first deacons were chosen. It is interesting to note that the second qualification (of only three) was to be *full* of the Spirit. How striking that the apostles assumed people would be able to know if someone was "full of the Spirit."

By the time we arrive at Acts 8 we see the results of one of these deacons living under the influence of the Spirit. Deacon Philip is now going to the city of Samaria to preach the gospel across racial and cultural lines, and the results are dramatic: people believed, many were baptized, healings and miracles took place, evil spirits came out of people, "and there was great joy in that city."[6]

You'd think that when the leaders back home in Jerusalem heard the reports they would have been content or even thrilled, but something crucial was missing—and it is this crucial something that distinguishes the early disciples from contemporary disciples in a very striking way.

As soon as they heard the Samaria story, an alarm went off in their hearts. All of this kingdom activity was amazing, but it was not enough. Immediately they sent Peter and John to Samaria to complete what was lacking in order to set these new believers up for kingdom fullness.

What did they do? They "prayed for them that they might receive the Holy Spirit. For as yet he had fallen upon none of them. They had only been baptized in the name of the Lord Jesus."[7] *Only?* Only been baptized in the name of Jesus? Only been born from above? Only been healed and delivered? Only changed the climate of a pagan city and brought great joy under the proclamation of the gospel?

Are we suggesting that the finished work of Jesus Christ is insufficient? Absolutely not. We don't need a new Savior but we need to go all the way with the Savior we have, and He has called us to encounter the fullness of the Spirit. Chief among the realities made possible because of the Gospel is that ordinary people can now become partakers of the divine nature and drink of the Holy Spirit.

He himself is the One who said, "It is to your advantage that I go away so that the Holy Spirit will come."[8] I have a hard time believing that there is a better option than having Jesus physically present in the room, physically engaged in our business, and physically involved in our trials, yet Truth himself said it is so. The Spirit activated in our real life is better than Jesus in the flesh. It is hard to believe, but it is only hard because we have settled for such a dumbed-down, natural version of our faith.

SEALED & FILLED

A word of explanation is in order. First, every believer *has* the Holy Spirit living inside of him or her. "Because you are sons, God has sent forth the Spirit of his Son into your hearts, crying out, 'Abba, Father!'"[9] "And it is God who... put his seal on us and has given us his Spirit in our hearts as a guarantee."[10] We never cease being *sealed* with the Spirit. However, we are not always *filled* with the Spirit. This is why Paul says in Ephesians 1:13 that all believers were sealed with the Holy Spirit, but then four chapters later he says to "not be drunk with wine... but be filled with the Holy Spirit."[11]

It's like trying to find sweet tea in New England. If you live in the southeastern United States you grow up on a beverage that is a cross between syrup and heaven: heavy on the sweet, mild on the tea. But when you travel north and ask for sweet tea, the waitresses condescendingly hand you packets of sugar to pour into your very cold iced tea. If you're southern, you understand why it takes 18 packets to make it taste like your grandmother's. If you're a chemist you understand why the sugar will not melt. But if you want the sugar to have its effect you learn very quickly how to make the drink work: you have to briskly stir it up, again and again. Your tea shall receive power when the sugar is stirred. Why? The stirring produces heat and it is through heat, that change happens.

The apostles knew what they were doing in Acts 8. It is entirely possible to be forgiven, baptized, on mission, and on your way to heaven—but still live a life that is less than filled. It is entirely possible to put a glass of tea to your lips and never utilize the sugar's power to make your taste buds sing, all because you did not stir. You stayed cold.

You can be absolutely *sealed* with the Spirit (which speaks to your positional reality), while remaining *unfilled* with the Spirit (which speaks to your practical reality). Being sealed is the once-and-for-all-reality of a soul adopted by God. It is glorious and precious and comforting, but it is not the same thing that Acts describes when the Spirit "falls upon" a believer when they are filled. Like a pilot light on a stove, the flame does not go out, but if you ever want to boil an egg, you'll need more than a pilot light. The fire is there all along; but it must be activated.

So many believers are asking all the wrong questions about the Holy Spirit. Cut through all the abstractions. Have you been filled with the Spirit? Have you turned up the flame lately? Or do you complacently sit back, proud of the fact that you can describe the finer points of pilot light theology? We encounter far too many missional Christians who have boldly embraced the call to go, penetrate culture, and invade darkness. Yet they have never actually been *filled* with the Spirit, or if they have, they have not continued to pursue that reality.

There is no such thing as once-filled-always-filled. These apostolic leaders were on to something that we might need to rediscover. We are most different when we are under the influence of the Holy Spirit. Our leadership is different when we lead under the influence. Our churches are different when we are moved under the influence. Our words are different when we speak under the influence. Ask until you receive.

EXPERIENCE

The apostle Paul compared being filled with the Spirit to coming under the influence of alcohol. What a curious comparison. Have you ever noticed that drunk people are often bolder than sober people? They step out. They take risks. They don't seem to fear failure. This is why so many rhythm-challenged guys need to get drunk before hitting the dance floor. No wonder so many Christians have such a hard time sharing their faith. It's not that they are not sincere; they are not filled.

Drunk people tolerate pain differently: it's almost as if they do not feel it (at least in the moment). Christians who regularly experience the infilling of the Holy Spirit are able to handle pain differently. It's not denial. It's different. You suffer differently when you are filled.

Drunk people even encounter a version of fellowship that is often inaccessible without the help of the drink. They say things they never would have said otherwise. They share what's on their mind; they remove the filters and open up their soul. They lower their inhibitions under the influence of the alcohol. It's ironic that many missional believers feel like if only they will go out and have a few drinks their friends may respond. The drinks may be irrelevant, but the Spirit is irreplaceable. Don't get drunk, be filled.

What if we became disciples who actually experienced the God we say we believe in? What if we went so deep in the Gospel that we did more than repeat the proclamation, but lived it's implications? Perhaps our testimony would sound less like a timeshare salesman describing a condo that they never visit, and more like a tour guide inviting people into the adventure that they are experiencing. There is nothing quite like being in the presence of a person in the process of tasting and seeing that the Lord is good.

We both love Dr. Pepper. We believe Dr. Pepper exists. We can describe Dr. Pepper. We could do the research and give a talk about the history, benefits, and glories of Dr. Pepper. But Dr. Pepper was not meant to be described; it was meant to be experienced. How tragic that so many Christians live out an experience with God that is loaded with information and yet often devoid of "taste and see."

Do you understand how much differently we process information under the influence of the Spirit? Do you understand how distinctly we speak when we are under the influence of the Spirit? It is always an exercise in futility when we try to do in the flesh what can only be done in the Spirit. He helps in our prayer. He helps in our mission. He helps in our weaknesses. Seek until you find.

FUTILITY OF THE FLESH

There is more at stake here than we realize. Our lack of regular Spirit experience is a source of untold frustration. So many biblical mandates are utterly impossible outside of a Spirit-empowered reality. If you've ever read the New Testament, you realize that many of the requirements of Jesus make the old covenant commands sound like "little league" in comparison. How in the world would God ever expect us to bless our enemies, heal the sick, love our spouse the same way Christ loves, or do greater works than Jesus? Going all the way in the path of Jesus is impossible, unless we live under the influence.

This is why by Acts 19, Christians had landed on this question. Did you receive the Spirit when you believed? It's the game-changer, and it is uncanny that there has not been a stronger emphasis on the Spirit among missional movements of Christians. Whether we bring to mind the promise of power for witness in Acts 1, or Jesus' self-declared mission to the poor and oppressed in Luke 4, the common denominator is the Spirit.

According to Scripture, the greatest gift we can bring to the poor, blind, afflicted, or lost is a ministry directly tied to the power of the Spirit.

A pastor friend recently shared about his fairly successful and growing church. He explained that at one time he had been quite open to the activity of the Holy Spirit in his ministry, but because he had become more missional, he felt the need to tone it down for the sake of reaching outsiders. He expressed his desire to create environments that are more predictable than many of his previous church experiences, for the sake of never making a guest feel uncomfortable. I walked away uneasy at the thought that predictability is perceived to be a missional tool.

We're not even sure that predictability and the way of Jesus can coexist. What seemed to mark Jesus and his followers throughout the gospels and into the book of Acts was a characteristic unpredictability. Take away the surprise, wonder, and mystery from our faith and we're left with an impotent religion. A. W. Tozer was correct, culture has put out the light in the souls of men and women. It has knocked the wind out of humanity, and that is precisely where we come in. We are people of the Spirit. The Scriptural word is *pneuma*, the word that describes wind. How exactly can somebody control or predict the wind?

Consider one of the more divisive and misunderstood manifestations of the Spirit: speaking in tongues. We bring this up as a concrete example, but also as a metaphor for all things Spiritual. To the onlooking world, much of what we do in the kingdom of God feels like another language entirely. The specific instructions regarding the use of this gift are found in 1 Corinthians 14, but one of the key points is this: if you speak in tongues while gathered as the church, it must be interpreted. Why? Because unexplained experiences like these cause confusion. It is not loving, and it is certainly not missional to go public with an experience that has no potential to build up the people around you.

However, if it *is* interpreted, it functions like a prophecy, which has a very different effect: the outsider is "convicted by all", the secrets of his heart are disclosed, and so, falling on his face, he will worship God and declare, "God is really among you."[12]

The Christian community itself is so divided on the issue that most people avoid the subject completely. What a shame. We find believers that either theologically or practically live in a way that leaves the experience of the Spirit confined to the pages of Scripture. Our creeds affirm that we believe in God the Holy Spirit, but if we are honest, we feel much more comfortable talking about the Father and the Son. The Spirit scares us. But notice that the apostle Paul assumes that our gatherings will include both outsiders *and* unique manifestations of the Holy Spirit. He does not tell them to tone it down; he simply calls them to explain what is going on every step of the way. Spiritual gifts were meant to convince sinners, not confuse them, while simultaneously building up believers. It is the genius of God to create a kingdom where the church's renewal is actually found as it participates in its very mission.

We contend that outsiders are not nearly as intimidated by the work of the Spirit as many Christians seem to think. What a disaster to witness so many churches respond to a spiritually curious culture by becoming increasingly secular and predictable. I confess that I feel the stress when I'm in a gathering where Christians begin to display their "oddness" in the midst of outsiders. If I'm honest, I get nervous when the wind starts to blow. I'm tempted to shut the doors and windows to return to normalcy, but time after time I have discovered that outsiders are far more open and ready than I thought. They've tried everything else. What if they are ready for something unpredictable?

Outsiders can handle the ways in which we are different, they just need an explanation. The answer to a flesh-obsessed culture is not a Spirit-diluted church. I find it ironic that the context of the oft-quoted warning in 1 Corinthians 14:40 ("all things should be done decently and in order") is the verse that precedes it: "Earnestly desire to prophesy and do not forbid to speak in tongues."[13] If we're honest, most of the Christian world functionally stresses one of these approaches to the exclusion of the other.

As far as this world is concerned we speak another language. Yes, we are from another country. They don't mind; they just need the interpretation. They *want* the interpretation in ways they cannot even explain. This chapter is a plea to reclaim the true essence of our tribe. We are the people of the Spirit. Knock until the door is opened.

APPLICATION

"Ask and it will be given to you; seek and you will find; knock and the door will be opened... If you then, who are evil, know how to give good gifts to your children, how much more will the heavenly Father give the Holy Spirit to those who ask him!"[14] It really is a fascinating promise, but it is a promise that the early Christians clearly tapped into. How do we respond to the promise of the Father?

Ask for the Holy Spirit. If you personally are not sure if you've ever been filled with the Holy Spirit, now is the time to ask. If you have been filled before, today is the day to be refilled, refreshed, and re-empowered. If you are a leader, I challenge you to begin "opening the window to allow the wind to blow in" to whatever it is that you lead. Ask for the Holy Spirit in the midst of decisions. If you are a pastor or microchurch leader, I encourage you to carve out space in your gatherings where you give the Spirit a chance to do His thing.

IMAGINE

Can you imagine what would happen if we began to ask for the Spirit again? What might happen if Bible teachers decided that they will not get up to teach unless they are filled? What if microchurch leaders embraced the call to be filled every time they shepherded their flock? Can you imagine going to a microchurch where every member came full enough to pour into others? Imagine being led by leaders who did not make final decisions until they were filled. What if missional Christians loved the poor enough to bring them ministry fueled by a true Spirit-overflow and not just the reserves of a weary soul. Imagine if arguing couples stopped talking, left the room and got filled with the Spirit before resuming the conversation. What might that do to a marriage?

We already do this by accident. Many of us have stumbled into a Spirit experience in the midst of corporate worship, during a particularly engaging quiet time, or in the middle of an especially edifying conversation. I am not calling us to something with which we have no experience whatsoever, but I want to be clear: I'm calling us to become intentional about something we can not quite put our finger on. I'm challenging us to go all the way with the Gospel we say we believe, because somewhere in the middle of this good news is the now-accessible presence and power of the Spirit. I'm asking us to be humble enough to recognize that we have been different than our early brothers and sisters in the faith—in the wrong kind of way.

What if we started asking the Spirit questions more often? Did you receive the Spirit when you believed? Were you filled with the Spirit to go into this meeting? Will we wait for the Spirit before engaging in ministry?

IMAGE

"Let us make man in our image..."[15] It wasn't the dust, fingers, or kneecaps that reflected the divine image. It was the invisible part, the breath of life. It was the Spirit. Because we were made for so much more than we can see or taste or touch. We were made for more than flesh.

We were made for deeper realities, and deeper purposes. When humans walked away from God, the deeper things went dormant and the flesh began to rule. The dust was never meant to be our defining characteristic. When we live by what can be tasted and touched alone we settle for a diminished existence, something less than the full life. We settle for dust, and we try to cover it up.

We miss the "ruach." It's the Hebrew word for wind, spirit, breath. This is not a call to ignore the physical. Biblical faith does not get caught up in the error of condemning all things physical and elevating all things spiritual. Jesus never calls us to simply pursue the invisible and ignore the earthly, but He is calling us to be fully human. Made of dust, but defined by His breath of life.

When they bit into the forbidden fruit, they really did die. They became fractured; alive, but dead. Human, but less than. Dust, without ruach. We've all eaten the fruit, and we've been missing something we can't put our finger on. We lost our ruach, and we've been trying to catch our breath ever since. That's why the problem has never just been the dust we were made from. Dust without ruach is what the Scripture means when describing what we call the sinful flesh, and this is why the best news we've ever received was when God took on flesh. What the first Adam lost, the second Adam is restoring. Fully God, fully man. Recapturing the original intent: made of dust, but defined by his breath of life.

We must rediscover and re-embrace our identity as people of the Spirit. I want us to humbly acknowledge the striking difference of the early Christians in their approach to the Spirit. Even our faithful disciples are often too fleshly, natural, and predictable to ever fulfill the world-changing desires of their hearts. We set ourselves up for frustration by casting vision and aspiring toward ends that will only be accomplished within the context of a true Spirit experience. A stuffy world dominated by flesh needs the difference that only comes from people who open themselves up to the animating breath of life. There is so much more available, if we will just ask. So ask, and then keep on asking for the Spirit. This reality will animate our lives, empower our mission, and change our communities.

ONE
TWO
THREE
FOUR
FIVE
SIX
SEVEN
EIGHT
NINE
TEN
ELEVEN
TWELVE

Boredom, Stools, and the Search for Wonder

How we talk about God matters, because we are all preach-
ers. All of us have a message and are responsible not only for
its content, but the heart behind it. Heartless communication
betrays the depth of the person we are trying to reveal. For
whatever reason God chooses to use people to reveal himself,
and we use words to reveal our hearts. When Jesus is our mes-
sage we should speak with a commensurate gravity and wonder.

Your message must match your life, but you still need a message. When we talk about preaching we don't just mean from a pulpit, we mean the spirit of prophecy and the hunger to faithfully hear and repeat the life-giving words of God. We affirm the role of dialogue, conversation, inquiry, and listening in mission and evangelism. All of these are essential, even critical in their own way. Still, *all* healthy people should practice these things, and we certainly should not neglect them, yet preaching is the unique domain of the Christian. We are supposed to have a message that when the conversation bends toward a hunger for the truth, we have something to say.

Mysteriously, preaching is still very much a staple of the modern worship experience. It seems to fly in the face of a kind of techno-centric trend away from seemingly outmoded forms of communication. Preaching is still relevant because God has chosen to be known in this primary way: hearing the good news preached.[1]

We believe that preaching not only still holds a place in the life of the church, but that it stands defiantly unchanged because of its importance in the life of the body. Still, not all preaching is created equal. Part of the reason why consumerism has swept into American churches like a plague is because a lot of the preaching proffered by our churches is so bad. This is a double-edged sword. When so much of our gathering's program is dependent on an ancient form of communication, you had better be able to do it well.

Figuring out what is good or bad preaching is itself a kind of puzzle. In a mad rush to be better than the other guy down the street, preachers often pander to their audiences, using parlor tricks, props, elaborate sets, and banal humor to get an edge on the competition. This breaks our hearts. On the one hand, we resolutely maintain the critical place of preaching in the life of the church. On the other hand, we have to challenge what passes for modern preaching and invite all of us—both speakers and listeners—into a more discerning ambition for what preaching can be.

For both of us, preaching is mostly about the heart. It is about the heart of God being communicated to the hearts of people through the heart of one leader. Too much of the stuff we are subjected to is heartless. If the speaker is not moved by what they are saying, if it has not gripped them with conviction or wonder, or overwhelmed their heart with gratitude or love, then it is less than true. It is not worthy of their audience.

All Scripture is God-breathed, and when we interpret or moderate the reading of Scripture, that breath must flow through us to our people. If you are not moved by that wind, animated by that spirit, and filled with that breath, then sit down. A less skilled speaker who is moved by what they are saying is infinitely more valuable (and even easier to listen to) than an expert who is pleased with themselves or who thinks what they are communicating is old hat. The kiss of death in preaching is to speak from old notes. There has to be life, and some aspect of novelty. We have to teach from the cutting edge of our awareness of God. Wonder is contagious and so is hypocrisy.

THE MUSIC WE HEAR

When Paul talked about his motivation for preaching there is a strange element of constraint in his description, as if he really had no choice. Consider this revealing and yet enigmatic passage:

> For when I preach the gospel, I cannot boast, since I am compelled to preach. Woe to me if I do not preach the gospel! If I preach voluntarily, I have a reward; if not voluntarily, I am simply discharging the trust committed to me. What then is my reward? Just this: that in preaching the gospel I may offer it free of charge...[2]

There is something going on in Paul that seems all too rare today. He feels compelled--as if it is involuntary--to preach, and yet that compulsion is not self-fulfilling. He cannot boast or claim a reward except that he has preached *without* reward, that he has offered his message without gaining anything from the enterprise.

The bit that most intrigues us about this passage, that we most want to understand and embody personally in preaching is the phrase "if not voluntarily." He is saying he cannot help himself. Not long ago I (Brian) was working late at the computer in my bedroom. To keep alert I turned on an Arctic Monkeys album and gave it some volume. My youngest son Skyler was lounging nearby in my bed, not sleeping but starting that slow decent. Like all good songs there was strong deliberate build up, as the bass line drove the song toward the inevitable crescendo. As I typed, my head started bobbing, and then I looked over towards the bed. There I saw my shirtless two-year old stand up on the bed, diaper drooping, his syncopated head nodding to the beat. I nodded back, and we keep time together, locking eyes in wordless agreement: this song is good. Then, as the song marched on, without breaking eye contact with me, his hand landed on his hip and a subtle hip motion was added to his impromptu dance. As the guitars came storming in with the chorus he dived headlong into the middle of the bed, rolled onto his side (still maintaining eye contact with me, mind you) and propping up his head with his left hand, he started raising and lowering his right leg in perfect time with the song. It was one of those truly hilarious moments that litters the landscape of parenthood, but I understood exactly what was going on. We probably all do.

Good music—the best music, the kind you really love—gets into you. Great music moves us, almost involuntarily. Great music can even move wallflowers from the sidelines to the dance floor. Whatever you were doing before is tabled, a memory subjected to the urgency of the music. If you have ever heard someone at a party scream, "That's my jam!" as they rush the dance floor, then you know what Skyler and I were feeling—perhaps even what Paul was feeling.

This gospel is the music I hear, and I have to move to it. Being able to hear it is its own reward. It is so beautiful, so engrossing, that I have to move to it. This text in Romans comes in the middle of an argument about freedom. In context, this is a counter-example to freedom. He is saying, I am free to eat, drink, or whatever, but when I hear this music, I want to and *have* to dance. Its rhythms supersede and govern my movements because I realize I was made for this. Once I heard this news, I knew that God made me for this music; to listen to it, move to it, and sing with it. God made me for preaching. "Woe to me," he says, as if he believes he will suffer if he does not preach, if he does not move to the music he hears.

When we communicate about God, whether from a stage, in a living room, or at the water cooler, it should seem uncontainable. We try too hard to act nonchalant in our communication about God, perhaps because we are afraid we will overwhelm people, but the message will be less true if it is not communicated with the gravity it deserves.

WHY WE DON'T LIKE STOOLS

There is a rash of young communicators that have put some faith in the stool to help them. They have wrongly believed that sitting on a stool will communicate warmth, winsome wisdom, and symbolize a conversational style. Of course, these kinds of props are not wrong in themselves, but they betray a wrong-headedness about preaching itself. Is preaching just a conversation? Is it meant to be warm wisdom dispensed by the sage at fireside? When we really think about preaching, or better yet think of the times we have heard preaching that has changed or altered the course of our lives, was it like that? It may be a more accessible way to communicate with an audience, but is the goal of preaching accessibility? When we try to put the cookies on the bottom shelf so that everyone can get them, have we forgotten that we are not actually supposed to be serving cookies when we preach?

There is a gravity to preaching that is lost when we trivialize it. Preaching is meant to have weight and wonder. It is meant to bend the mind and awaken the soul. If we think of creating a conversation that dispenses pithy points for better daily living, then we have emasculated the actual intent of preaching.

Preaching at its heart is prophecy, not in the futuristic sense, but in the more normative biblical sense. It is an attempt to say the words of God to the people of God. Again, we look to a prophet like John the Baptist as an example. People were drawn to John, while he withdrew from people. He was a serious man with a serious life and a serious message. He knew that he was a messenger for God, and that task left him with little room in his life for the trivial or the trite. When Jesus talked about John he asked the revealing, if sarcastic question:

> What did you go out into the wilderness to see? A reed swayed by the wind? If not, what did you go out to see? A man dressed in fine clothes? No, those who wear fine clothes are in kings' palaces. Then what did you go out to see? A prophet? Yes, I tell you, and more than a prophet.[3]

What do people come to our churches to see? What do they come into our living rooms in our Christian communities to see? A reed swayed by the wind? Someone who is cool and dresses right? The longing heart is always longing for God. The voice people want to hear is God's.

And while Jesus often taught with stories and human metaphors, his listeners were never at a loss for whose voice they had just heard. When groping for words to describe the tenor of his teaching, the only word that people could agree on was authority. This is what prophecy is: authoritative words, not warming words, or proverbial thoughts made plain for the common man, but words with the weight of the voice of God behind them.

Can you imagine John the Baptist preaching from a stool? Words like his cannot be rightly delivered while sitting. We stand when we preach because we are too animated by the depth and weight of the work we are entering into to sit. We stand when we preach because of the reverence for the words and the will behind those words we are trying to represent. We stand when we preach because we are ourselves equally at attention, listening to the voice of God, ready to respond in obedience and joy.

Maybe this exposes a way in which we are different. We do not see God primarily as a tool for life. As if meeting and knowing Jesus, reading the Bible, or being a part of a church is a way of living a slightly better life than everyone else. As if we make an appeal to people who are looking for self-improvement or common wisdom by inviting them into a relationship with Jesus.

If you enter into a relationship with Jesus, you become his. Your life is no longer your own. This is orthodox Christianity, to invite people into a self-improvement program consisting of bible reading and occasional self-centered prayer is to teach heresy. Orthodox Christianity has always been about recognizing the supremacy of Jesus Christ in your life as in all things. Consider the first question and response of the Heidelberg Catechism: "What is your only comfort in life and death? That I am not my own, but belong with body and soul, both in life and in death, to my faithful Savior Jesus Christ."

Our preaching must communicate that kind of submission. Preaching that carries no authority cannot in turn carry this kind of message. It is simply not possible. Many catering super-churches have wrongly believed that we must simplify and moderate the radical claims of the gospel in order to lure and win the seeker. The problem then is that the seeker is led to believe that this is the gospel, that the message of Jesus and his kingdom is a moderate's path and one that requires very little investment. Only later when they read the words of Jesus for themselves will they discover a dissonance with what they have been taught. In our experience, people are not actually attracted to Jesus when his message is moderated. They may be attracted to a quasi-committed Christianity, but it is not Jesus they are drawn too—and in Mike's case he has come to discover that an un-compromised message that carries authority and humility actually can still attract people by the thousands.

IT IS A SIN TO BORE THEM

We have always loved the missional focus and clarity of Young Life with their passion for lost high school kids. One of their organizational mantras that every staff must live by is, "It is a sin to bore a kid". Perhaps too often that conviction has been translated into an unspoken mantra "therefore entertain them," but I think at the heart of this commitment is not the desire to entertain but to captivate. Counter-intuitively, their conviction places the responsibility of boredom on the missionary, not the kids, which is provocative at least and perhaps even revolutionary. Regardless of who is responsible for the boredom of the listener, it is right to identify boredom as an enemy of effective mission.

Peter Toohey, in his thrilling and thought provoking book 'Boredom, A Lively History,' argues that boredom comes from repetition and confinement.[4] Shockingly, this seemingly innocuous experience actually produces some of our most dangerous emotions; anger, depression and disgust (boredom is to disgust what frustration is to anger). This may not be something we have thought through, but just try and remember the last time you were profoundly bored—perhaps it was in church—and you will recall feeling these very same emotions.

The experience of boredom is like the slowing of time. It is the psychological torture of monotony and confinement. When we are truly and completely bored, we tend to compare the experience to dying, saying we are "bored to death." While hyperbole, this is not completely untrue as it relates to preaching. When we are bored in the presence of the church we are experiencing a kind of spiritual death.

Boredom has always been a part of the Christian experience but only as a temptation of the desert, in solitude, and extended prayer. The desert was a place of confinement and repetition, and ultimately a place of temptation. The fourth century desert father Evagrius, in his work called 'On the Eight Evil Thoughts' names what he calls "acedia," or the noonday demon.[5] In his description, it is hard not to rename the noonday demon the demon of boredom. Boredom opens us to temptation, because what we feel in the throes of boredom is actually disgust. In that disgust with the fruitlessness of that moment or even our lives as a whole we are open to something that is more appealing and that promises to release dopamine into our brains. One study revealed that 52% of teenagers are at risk of using drugs if they have one of the three characteristics: stress, boredom, or too much money.

However, Toohey argues that boredom is actually a *good* emotion, precisely because it produces anger and even disgust. It becomes a healthy catalyst to unhealthy repetition or confinement. Boredom can save us from complacency; a yawn is not a sign of sleep but instead actually a sign of *fighting* sleep, increasing the blood flow to a tiring brain. The yawn is our body's attempt to antagonize sleepiness. Maybe spiritual boredom is in the same way meant to antagonize apathy, spiritual idleness, and inactivity.

Disgust protects us from disease and things that could be dangerous to us. Research shows that people find a towel with a brown stain more disgusting than a towel with a blue stain. This sense of disgust protects us from hidden but potentially very real danger. Boredom is the disgust of confinement and repetition without reason. Maybe we are spiritually disgusted with ourselves to protect us from something that is spiritually dangerous.

If you have ever felt bored in prayer, you know that there is a temptation to think you must be doing it wrong, or to just assume that your faith is weak because your attention span seems so short, but perhaps that boredom is not a bad thing. Maybe it is God letting you know to shake it up; not to stop praying, but to pray differently. What if God is bored too? What if that disgust you feel is meant to make you wake up and change something?

I can remember being so bored in church services and feeling like something must be wrong with me. I was recently at a conference where I had to sit through what felt like an eternity of talks. It was really just one full day, but it felt like psychological torture. My point being that I still wrestle with the noonday demon, but what if that boredom is not evil at all?

Maybe church was meant to be more than what we see, and maybe the listener is not the problem. Maybe boring an audience while talking about the marvel that is Jesus Christ is a sin and an offense to his beauty. Perhaps that disgust is a warning light going off in my heart because God is greater than heartless drivel.

What about when we feel bored with ourselves? Maybe God made us for adventure, and life was meant to be something it currently isn't. Maybe we are not testing ourselves, and maybe the disgust we feel is with the lameness of our lives and the truce we have called with mediocrity. What if the part of us that longs for God, the part of us that used to dream, the part of us that once walked under the miraculous cloud by day and the pillar of fire by night, the part of us that walked through a parted sea from the hands of certain death, what if that part is screaming out from the deepest place in our soul: "There is more. You were meant for more!"

The disgust and torture of boredom is really a gracious reminder to look for something more. Our deepest spiritual crisis can be described as boredom, and this kind of existential boredom is what St. John of the Cross called the 'dark night of the soul'. It creates a sense of emptiness, isolation, disgust, and waywardness. Whether it is ordinary boredom or existential boredom, I do believe that the sense of unfulfilled longing offers honest data about whatever is causing the crisis, and I am convinced that prolonged exposure to ordinary boredom in a church setting eventually creates existential boredom as we question the deepest things of God in the tedious, lifeless settings of church done wrong.

Personally, I (Brian) am intimately acquainted with boredom. Diagnosed as hyperactive as a child, I struggled to ever sit still. My one sibling, an older sister, was constantly the victim of my unending quest to stave off boredom. I can remember feeling so tortured by boredom that I would do anything to break out. I invented a game where I would knock on my poor sister's door over and over (imagine 100 knocks at your door) as she did her best to ignore me. Eventually, infuriated, she would swing open the door in a rage and knock me down. I would walk away bruised and happy, only to return five minutes later to start again.

Some of the stupidest things I have ever done I did because I was bored, including (but not limited to) jumping off our roof with an umbrella, and trying to light fireworks by pouring a line of gun powder leading up to them (a caper that actually burned off my eyebrows). However, boredom also pushed me towards some of the smartest things I've done, too. I ran for class president because I was bored with school. I played high school sports. I learned to use tools, and how to take apart a bike and put it back together. I invented elaborate games, and was in constant ergonomic research and development of the best arrangement of my room.

If boredom at its best is a warning light about the trajectory of a course of action or situation and a clue to an unfulfilled longing, then boredom in preaching has to make us look for change.

MAKE US WONDER

The life and ministry of Jesus before and after the ascension was characterized by amazement, not only for the disciples but for all who were watching and listening. Jesus' words and actions brought people to wonder:

> When Jesus had finished saying these things, the crowds were amazed at his teaching, because he taught as one who had authority, and not as their teachers of the law.[6]

> And when the demon was driven out, the man who had been mute spoke. The crowd was amazed and said, "Nothing like this has ever been seen in Israel."[7]

> The people were amazed when they saw the mute speaking, the crippled made well, the lame walking and the blind seeing. And they praised the God of Israel.[8]

> The men were amazed and asked, "What kind of man is this? Even the winds and the waves obey him!"[9]

> So again Pilate asked him, "Aren't you going to answer? See how many things they are accusing you of."[10]

> But Jesus still made no reply, and Pilate was amazed.[11]

> Utterly amazed, they asked: "Are not all these men who are speaking Galileans? Then how is it that each of us hears them in his own native language?[12]

> Amazed and perplexed, they asked one another, "What does this mean?"[13]

The antithesis of boredom is not adrenaline. It is wonder.

The preacher is a worship leader. The goal is not to thrill or entertain but to stun people with the brilliance of Jesus and cause them to worship him on the spot. This is why Paul "decided to know nothing among you except Jesus Christ and him crucified." We hope our words will lead those who listen to a place where only God can meet them. It is to take them to the edge of the Grand Canyon and then to simply stand there with them, breathless. There are two connotations to the word 'wonder' and both are appropriate. First is to question or puzzle over something, as in,

"I wonder what that means." The other is to marvel, to experience the speechlessness of awe and to stare in wonder. Why does so much modern preaching lack both of these connotations? There is no puzzling and there is no awe in the presentation, only puffed up certainty that lacks the humility and respect that someone talking about God should carry.

My (Brian) favorite art gallery in the world is the Tate Modern in London. Every time I am in London I try to go. I am challenged by the lack of boundaries in modern art, and of course the Tate building itself is a work of art (and it's also free). I like modern art because part of what you have to do when you look a piece is wonder, "What is it?" Sometimes I will sneak in on a tour and listen to the guide explain a piece. What I think about it is usually pretty unsophisticated, but then to hear the story behind the piece and the artist reveals how there is always so much more to see and know. I start with wonder in the first sense, "I wonder what this piece means," and end with wonder in the second sense, "wow". This is what a good sermon should do, or even a good *conversation* for that matter. It should start with a question that matters, and end with a revelation. You have no way of knowing what will or will not be a revelation to your audience, but you know what is to you. Our message should always build an altar (a place to come and sacrifice ourselves to God), and we should be the first one to come and bow there.

Again Paul leads us, "I will not venture to speak of anything except what Christ has accomplished through me..."[14] Talk about the things that are personally real to you, the truths that you embody, full of personal meaning and wonder. We are not advocating more entertaining preaching. We are advocating zeal, honesty, sincerity and the honest pursuit of God in the message we carry. If you talk about God to other people in any context, we plead with you to make sure that it comes from a place of real relationship and wonder.

If you find what you are talking about beautiful, challenging, fascinating, and captivating, so will your audience. Tell the story of your own relationship with God. Be in awe of the one to whom you are referring to, and I promise we will not be bored—and if you are boring people, then lock yourself in the place of prayer until you see that the one for whom you speak is unspeakably beautiful.

ONE
TWO
THREE
FOUR
FIVE
SIX
SEVEN
EIGHT
NINE
TEN
ELEVEN
TWELVE

"WHY DO YOU CALL ME, 'LORD, LORD,'
AND DO NOT DO WHAT I SAY?"
LUKE 6:46

Commission, Kids, and the Kingdom Come

The final exhortation from us has to be related to the final exhortation of Jesus. His parting words to his students carry a special significance because they invite us all to become spiritual parents and to take part in the work and joy of kingdom reproduction.

So much of our discussion so far requires imagination. There are precious few examples of all these qualities in one person or one community, but they do exist. There are fewer Christians in our world than the statistics say, but they are there nevertheless, and these odd, holy, different people are a precious commodity. When a real disciple is formed, they become the key to growth, health, and culture in the new generation of the church and the future of mission in the world. That is not just hyperbole; even a small group of authentic disciples can change the world if they listen and obey the words Jesus gave that first small group of authentic disciples on that mountain in Galilee.

We call it the Great Commission, and it *is* a commission. But it is *also* an invitation to all the things we have mentioned in this book. Those final instructions are pregnant with meaning, touching on authority, grace, empowerment, embodiment, preaching, the Spirit, and finally intimacy. The mission they are given is meant to multiply their discipleship in the world. That mission is also meant to anchor them, forever binding them to Jesus. The commission is for the world, but it is for them too because making disciples is not just the work of the church it is our joy as well.

BE FRUITFUL AND MULTIPLY

Again, we have 14 children between us, so reproduction hits pretty close to home. We often experience the joy of looking into the eyes of another human that clearly bears our physical image. We also encounter the horror of watching a child reproduce words, attitudes, and perspectives that we would like to forget. It's a sobering truth: our lives are already reproducing *something;* the question is what?

We have been friends for a very long time. We first met on a first-grade field trip, and became inseparable when we were freshmen in high school. We have walked together through our whole adult lives, but have not always embodied the ideas we have offered here. At 15, we started a Bible club at our school on Friday mornings, but usually skipped class as soon as it was over. Our lives would have certainly carried an R-rating as Mike had a weakness for girls and Brian for fighting and foul language. We were full of contradictions, but something happened to both of us during our time together in college. It was a work of the Holy Spirit and a work of holiness. We began to challenge the sameness and indifference of our faith. We began to take to heart the words and vision of the Great Commission. We looked at our lives and realized these were not the kind of lives that should be replicated, reproduced, or otherwise multiplied. That is why this chapter is last; even though it is perhaps the first and most important missional command of the church, there are some things we have to sort out in our lives before we reproduce them.

All these years later that fire that was lit inside of us has never died. God is faithful. We have dedicated the fullness of our lives and resources (as best we know how) to making disciples and glorifying the lover of our souls. And you may think we have a lot of natural born children, but we have so many more *spiritual* ones.

> All authority in heaven and on earth has been given to me. Go therefore and make disciples of all the nations, baptizing them in the name of the Father and of the Son and of the

Holy Spirit, teaching them to observe all that I have commanded you.[1]

It is really quite simple. The church is created to reproduce. The church is *commanded* to reproduce. We make disciples; not religious services, song lists, interesting sermons, or flow charts. On the day of judgment, every one of us will stand before God and give an account for our faithfulness to this command: Are we bringing disciples—Jesus-followers—with us into eternity? It is tragic that the average Christian has never intentionally "made" even one disciple.

"Make disciples" is the reproductive *what*. These modifying participles are the reproductive *how*: baptizing them, and teaching them to observe. While there is no such thing as a discipleship formula, the fundamental components are brilliantly summed up in these two mandates.

BAPTIZING

According to Jesus, reproduction demands a birth. Baptizing is the first side of the discipleship coin. What are we doing when we baptize people? We are making disciples. It is a profound error to separate a word like 'evangelism' from a word like 'discipleship.'

Let's take a step back and make a statement that strikes at the heart of a warped discipleship approach. Christians need to stop obsessing over "getting fed." In John 20, Jesus tells Peter to "feed [His] sheep," and we find this idea in Ezekiel 34 where God was speaking "against the shepherds of Israel" who failed to feed the sheep and instead fed themselves. "The weak you have not strengthened, the sick you have not healed, the injured you have not bound up, the strayed you have not brought back, the lost you have not sought... My sheep were scattered with none to search or seek for them..."[2]

Imagine the scene. Peter swims up to a beach where the Messiah he denied is cooking him breakfast over a charcoal fire. Just a few days earlier, he was warming himself around another charcoal fire when a girl gave him a chance to stand up for a suffering Jesus. He failed miserably, the cock crowed, and he fled in shame, lacking the belief in a redeemer who could beat death, much less his sin.

Peter now finds himself looking into the eyes of the Man he betrayed, with the smell of his failure in his nostrils. He then hears the question he never saw coming, with a command that would change his life: *Do you love me? Feed my sheep.* When most Christians hear the words *feed my sheep* they tend to think reaching in. Going deep. Finding a church that meets *my family's* needs. They call it *discipleship.* Which is why, for most people *feed my sheep* means improving existing believers, but we don't think that's what Peter heard.

There's no doubt that improving and caring for found sheep is part of what Ezekiel 34 had in mind. Strengthen the weak, heal the sick, have good inductive Bible studies; this is all good stuff, but when you read the story of Peter you do not find him staying *in;* he goes *out.* For Peter, evangelism and discipleship were not distinct activities. Central to God's rebuke to shepherds was their characteristic neglect of *lost* sheep.

After 2,000 years, Christians still miss it. We tend to think "feed my sheep" means preaching good sermons. We consider this the job of the teachers and shepherds, maybe a few prophets, and never the evangelist or apostle. We still believe "feed my sheep" means helping already-found sheep shine a little brighter, but what if it refers to the great commission? What if it's about making disciples?

What if the act of *feeding sheep* and *making disciples* is more like an urgent search for your lost keys when you're running late for work? Funny how we never hear people passively sitting down to rationalize theology with their lost keys. *Well, maybe I was predestined to never find these keys. If God wants me to have them, he'll find a way.* Let's be honest; if we treated looking for lost keys the way we treat looking for lost sheep, we'd be unemployed.

Since we have so many kids to look after, every now and then we lose one. Ruth and Monica don't seem to have this problem as much as we do. Can you imagine if one of us went home to our wife with a child missing? As she explodes with maternal concern, we couldn't get away with saying, "Calm down. We still have the rest of them. Let's not be all about numbers. Besides that, the more kids, the less the rest of us get our needs met. Having one less means more food and space for the rest of us. We don't want to be one of those television mega-families. We like small. All these extra people around the house make everything harder." Of course this wouldn't fly; these are her children. These are her sheep.

What if a cheating coworker of yours is Jesus' sheep, but he doesn't know it yet? What if your irritating neighbor is his sheep, but she's never been told? What if "feed my sheep" means we're rubbing shoulders with lost sheep all the time, but God is waiting for people with a heart like his who are willing to reproduce, which is why he's asking, *Do you love me?* Then go make disciples. We contend that making disciples is exactly what Jesus said it is: teaching *and* baptizing.

There is far too much ministry that is little more than what Paul described as building on another person's foundation. Most Christian ministry is really just a competition for a market share in the activity of improving the already reached. This is why Paul was committed to bringing the gospel where it had not yet gone, and this is why we sound the trumpet for a different approach to ministry, an original recipe. We call our people to give their lives to reach people who are not being reached, save people who are not being saved, and plant churches among people where the kingdom has yet to reproduce.

This is the essence of *baptizing*, and a call to live with such wisdom, passion, and hope that we are intentionally leading people across the line of faith. We fully recognize that salvation is of the Lord, and yet we know that he uses vessels. People cannot baptize themselves. The saltier we are, the thirstier they will be.

The joy of the harvest is not reserved for the select minority of Christians with a talent in persuasion. While every believer is not an evangelist, every believer can be evangelistic. In God's sovereignty, every Christian has a unique network of relationships and neighbors that nobody else will ever be able to touch.

While it is good to lead people to repent in prayer, the clear and pivotal moment for the early church was baptism (as evidenced in the book of Acts). Baptism is clear, an outward response to an inward reality, and that inward reality is this: *I'm all in. I repent from my sin and I repent toward my Savior. It is on Jesus' terms not mine. It is his righteousness, not mine. I trust Jesus.*

Every microchurch—and every disciple—should be praying to God for the privilege of baptizing the people in their lives. We pray for a healthy and holy burden for the souls of men and women, accompanied by prayers like the women of old: Lord, give us children. Reproduce new life through us.

TEACHING TO OBSERVE

The second component of our commission to reproduce is *teaching them to observe*. Think about the difference between a parent and your average teacher. The teacher is paid to comprehensively deliver the information while a parent will do whatever it takes until the child gets it. Their love leads them to have a vision for their child, and their vision leads them to work at the craft of child rearing. They read books about getting a child to sleep through the night, how to potty train, and when to affirm. Overachieving parents want their children to swim by age two, read by age three, and shoot a basketball by age four. Parents take this so seriously that they read the experts, scour the internet, and go to parenting seminars. Ultimately they take in all this information and customize a plan for their child.

We need to acknowledge something: we already make disciples. We teach children to brush their teeth, eat their food, speak with adults, and respond to our words. We live with them, talk to them, correct them, and reward them. We take them on trips and put them to bed; we sing them songs and tell them stories. Discipleship is spiritual parenting, but unfortunately we now seem to have a generation of spiritual orphans and latch-key kids being raised by the television. There are not many spiritual mothers or fathers anymore. We treat churches like boarding schools where we send our spiritual children off to be trained by the professionals. Lacking real parents, we have settled for charming babysitters and articulate hired hands.

How do spiritual mothers and fathers *teach them to observe?* It starts by simply *being.* Like reproduces like, fire will not reproduce ice, and distracted Christians will not reproduce focused disciples. Thus we need to live a life that is truly worth following, since so much of what we reproduce will be done accidentally. God is not mocked. A man reaps what he sows. If we sow seeds of prayer and generosity, for example, we will reap a harvest of prayer and generosity. If we sow seeds of greed and rage, we will likely reap a harvest of greed and rage.

Sages have pointed out that we can teach what we know, but we reproduce who we are. Yet this only happens if we become intentional. *Being* alone is not enough; we must embrace the *be-with* factor. The word must become flesh and the epistle must become living. This means we probably have to extend a clear invitation: *Come follow me as I follow Jesus.* This seems to be the consistent New Testament strategy for reproduction.

Paul said, "Keep your eyes on those who walk according to the example you have in us."[3] This sounds a lot like Hebrews 6:12: "Do not be sluggish, but be imitators of those, who through faith and patience inherit the promises." Paul tells Timothy, "Follow the pattern... that you have heard from me."[4] Herein lies the reproduction challenge. Most Christian ministries seem to expect discipleship and reproduction to be the result of good, solid Bible teaching, yet Paul embraced the paradigm of a spiritual father. This included instruction: "You... have followed my teaching..." But he did not stop there: "my conduct, my aim in life, my faith, my patience, my love, my steadfastness, my persecutions and sufferings that happened to me...",[5] Timothy got to see how Paul responded to victory, or defeat, or infirmity. He was able to observe what would thrill Paul's soul or drive him crazy. He heard him counsel and watched him wait. There is no doctrine as compelling as the one being lived out before your eyes.

Reproduction starts with an immersion in water, but it beckons people to the ongoing immersion into our lives. People must be invited to be *with* us to varying degrees. The lion's share of our discipleship is the result of people being consistently exposed to the intangibles of our lives. This is why we must invite people in and cast a vision of reproduction.

Think about the context of one of the more memorable conversations of the New Testament. "Who do the crowds say that I am?"[6] Peter, of course, shines when he makes the now famous confession, "You are the Christ."[7] Notice how the encounter begins: "Now it happened that, as he was praying *alone*, the disciples were *with him*."[8] *With* him. Is it possible that the prayer curiosity of Luke 11 ("Lord, teach us to pray...") is created by the exposure of episodes like Luke 9? It seems that Jesus did not merely have quiet times; he invited people *in* to his quiet times. Our lives have been deeply impacted by Jesus' great prayer of John 17, yet how did we come to have a transcript of that prayer? Jesus was praying *alone*, but John was *with him*.

Who is invited into the secret places of your life? A big part of reproducing is simply being there, but once you're there you need to connect the dots. This is where the role of *words* comes into play. There is probably nothing more pivotal for reproduction than the words that a disciple hears. Some of these words are spontaneous and casual; some of these words are premeditated and organized. All of these words are crucial.

Perhaps the greatest parenting passage in the Bible is found in Deuteronomy 6:6-7. "And these words that I command you today shall be on your heart." *Your* heart, mom and dad. This speaks to the *being* of the parent. "You shall teach them diligently to your children, and shall talk of them when you sit in your house, and when you walk by the way, and when you lie down, and when you rise." This points to the *be-with* factor, but it specifies a key activity when we are with our children: our speech.

Children are not raised in the predictability of a school classroom; they are reproduced in the comprehensive reality of an actual life. Sitting down. Walking around. Lying down. Getting up. In other words, Moses commanded the parents of Israel to find a way to verbally connect the dots between whatever is going on in the real world and the words of God.

Teach them to observe everything I have commanded you. Of course this can include an expository sermon and an inductive Bible study. Of course this might mean a weekly trip to a coffee shop for an in-depth one-on-one. But this will never be enough. Think back to the "private" prayer of Jesus. You don't reproduce mighty men and women of prayer by simply getting people to memorize the Lord's prayer. You have to be with *and* listen in on a person who talks to God like they know him. You can't teach people how to suffer well by simply listening to a sermon from James 1. You need to listen in on both what's going on and being said behind the scenes in the life of someone suffering well. You do not learn to seek first the kingdom by being told to do so, you pick this up when you spend time with people who live and breathe the kingdom whether they are at a football game or in a microchurch gathering. There is simply no substitute for watching and listening to a spiritual father or mother live a life of worship or mission. Spiritual parents make space to pray, eat, discuss, witness, and party *together.* Reproduction requires watching how the words of God intersect with real life, which is why these words must be in your heart.

This means we need to recognize the latent potential of ordinary places as discipleship holy ground. Discipleship with Jesus included the intimate moments with his inner circle as well as the public places among the noisy crowd. How did Jesus turn ordinary people into radical disciples? He turned ordinary situations into opportunities for transformation. Ordinary settings became holy spaces.

So often Jesus "began to teach beside the sea." Although the synagogue was the expected setting for a teacher, Jesus did it anywhere and everywhere. He was always reproducing; teaching was not separate from mission. There are so many opportunities that are not confined to the organized church and microchurch gatherings. It's about being in the right place at the right time, and seizing the moment by simply talking about Jesus and his word, wherever they might apply.

What might this look like? Is an athlete talking smack? That's a perfect moment to talk about the humility or silence of Jesus. Is traffic unusually heavy? Instead of checking our phone or pounding the steering wheel, we reproduce when talking about the work of patience in a disciple's life. Has a spiritual leader really blown it? It's a brilliant opportunity to demonstrate and verbalize sincere repentance. It's senseless for parents to expect their children to know how to repent well when they have never seen it done. Love, joy, peace, patience, these are the fruit of the Spirit, but they are reproduced through the people in whom He lives.

WHO TO CHOOSE

To whom do we direct our reproduction? How do we choose people? It is interesting to note that Jesus had a rather large number of loosely affiliated apprentices (disciples) before he whittled it down to the group of 12 through whom he intended to concentrate his focus. We sometimes feel like the first thing he did was to choose his 12, and then he got into the discipleship business, but there is quite a bit of action—and many months of observation— that transpired before Jesus finally made his apostolic decision in Luke 6. How serious was he? He continued "all night in prayer."[9] With limited relational time and energy, he knew that the mission collapses if there is not reproduction. He wanted hungry people, and he needed divine wisdom to identify such a trait. This is worth serious prayer and reflection.

Every good leader knows that training the unmotivated is an exercise in futility. We choose the hungry, the able, and the available. We pick people willing to pass the 2 Timothy 3:10 test (*follow my teaching, conduct, aim in life...*) Choose the people who are willing to do what you are doing. In an age of narcissism, Christians everywhere envision a discipleship paradigm that supplies them with a weekly counseling appointment where a mentor lets them talk about themselves for an hour. This is not reproduction. In fact, you are hard-pressed to find any record of Jesus doing a one-on-one with any of his apostles. While there is nothing wrong with such a meeting, this is a small blip on the radar of a life of reproduction. There must be real-life reproduction.

In John 12 we find an interesting encounter that makes the point in a strange way. Some Greeks heard about Jesus and came to his disciple Philip requesting a meeting. Philip tells Andrew, who tells Jesus about their request. Jesus' response seems out of place: "The hour has come for the Son of Man to be glorified. Truly, truly, I say to you, unless a grain of wheat falls into the earth and dies, it remains alone; but if it dies, it bears much fruit."[10] In other words, there will always be more needs knocking at the door than we will have the ability to meet. There is only one option: reproduce. And in some ways, reproducing will be like a little death; death to your privacy and death to your hidden agendas, death to your carefully preserved image. But if we will embrace the call, we will discover a joy that is related to the resurrection itself.

AS YOU GO

What does this look like in the real world? It is humbling to read the reports of how the church is exploding all over the world, primarily through the work of untrained lay people choosing lives of reproduction. Lacking the advantage of education and formal training, many movements are utterly dependent upon the principle of reproduction. They invite other disciples into the various slices of their lives, and they walk the journey together. It is life on life, whether that means parenting, church-planting, or visiting the sick. They *intentionally* do everything together, for the purpose of reproducing, and they are shaking the planet with their impact.

Discipleship reproduction must not become another list of tasks to accomplish in a week. Wisdom demands more and more overlap with the lives we are already living. Mothers will already be parenting their children, they just need to allow other women in. Parents are already eating meals with the children, why not steer the conversation toward the kingdom? We already go shopping. We just need to bring others along. We already engage in sports and hobbies, why not get intentional and do it with people we have seen to be fruitful?

Most people never get started because they feel so ill-equipped to do it, but discipleship and reproduction are a lot like tending a garden. There are some methods that produce more fruit than others, but the bottom line is this: gardens need attention. You do not learn to garden by incessantly reading about gardening. At some point, the fingernails just need to get dirty.

This is Jesus' strategy to change the world. Live a life worth sharing, and then share it. Get better and better at living this life, and get better and better at sharing this life. Microchurches need to create an environment worth sharing and then reproduce it. Teachers need to develop their craft and then reproduce what they know. Leaders need to make more leaders. Preachers need to make more preachers. Churches need to make more churches. We need fathers and mothers to reproduce generations.

We see a failure to do this tragically played out in the opening chapters of the book of 1 Samuel, where we meet a spiritual leader named Eli. While he possesses the authority and power of God, we are soon introduced to his sons, whom the author describes as "worthless,"[11] despite the position granted them by their father. As time goes by, God uses Eli to speak a word of blessing, which opens the womb of a barren woman. She calls her son Samuel, and gives him to God to be trained by Eli in the house of the Lord.

The boy grows to be strong in the things of God and establishes himself as the great prophet in Israel. Toward the end of his ministry, however, we see a familiar and tragic flaw. As he considers his succession, he gives his sons positions of spiritual leadership. "Yet his sons,"—just like Eli's—"did not walk in his ways, but turned aside after gain. They took bribes and perverted justice."[12] This becomes the proverbial straw that breaks the back, as the people of Israel then reject God as king, and demand a human king to rule instead.

Don't miss the lesson; while Eli reproduced a *prophet*, he never reproduced a *father*, and the results were heartbreaking. "It was the will of the Lord to put them to death."[13] The warning is clear. We either embrace a different approach and learn to reproduce or the movement dies. Like a seedless watermelon that is sweet to the taste but with nothing more to offer. It is but one generation of fruit, sweet and convenient, but very, very sterile.

We must embrace the call to reproduce generations of justice, righteousness, and wisdom. With enough natural talent, charisma, and good timing anybody can produce an attractive ministry or a temporarily effective missional endeavor, but we must be different. We must reproduce.

A NEW HERITAGE

I had a man approach me one day in response to an urgent missions need presented to our church family. He verbalized his intention to do something quite extravagant about the giving opportunity before him. I do not believe in talking people down while they are being prompted by the Spirit, but I had to make sure the man considered carefully what he was saying. This would require substantial sacrifice and courage on his part. With tears in his eyes, he looked me in the face, and told me the story of a childhood that had marked him forever. There were many variables, but the constant through it all was the unmistakable presence of the living God, and a father who believed him.

"I was raised by a man who refused to live by sight, and despite our occasional kicking and screaming, he walked us through the life of faith. We gave away money and cars and even a house, and Jesus never let us down." Then he paused. "This is my heritage."

This is where the church can be brilliant. In the midst of a generation which has never been fathered, can you imagine the impact of a movement of people who reclaim the ancient call to spiritually mother or father the children of God? I never cease to be moved by the raw compassion and devotion of the early church. Places like ancient Ephesus apparently had "baby dumps" where people discarded their unwanted newborns. It seemed to them more humane than allowing another unwanted child to wreak havoc on society, yet there are documents that suggest that early Christians would go and pull the babies out and adopt them as their own. The spirit of adoption has an effect on a soul. When you've been fathered by the King, it transforms the way you live.

ONE FINAL THOUGHT

There are certainly more lessons to learn and other facets of a holy life. These twelve meditations do not comprise a comprehensive discipleship curriculum, but they are some of what we think you need to know, in our time, to be different enough so that the reproduction of your way of life could actually change the world.

Part of what we are saying is that these themes are particularly important because we have not gotten them right, because so many of the cracks in the integrity of the church in our time and our culture can be traced back to a misunderstanding of these ideas. We do not think they are more important than other biblical themes, only that they are more timely—and therefore more significant—for us to address today.

We have to *really* understand the love and grace of God. So much is riding on that. We have to hold doggedly to the centrality of Jesus in our search for truth, community, and purpose. We have to learn again to pray, and know the God who calls and sends us. We have addressed the needs of the poor and the needy, or we are no representation of Jesus to this impoverished world. We have to learn again to serve in our leadership and give away power instead of abusing it. We have to live what we say, and say what we live. We have to give all of our lives and not play percentages with God. We must learn to listen and follow the leadership of the Spirit that God has given to empower and to comfort us. We must preach with our words and our lives—and finally, teach others to do the same.

When you see it all together you begin to understand the vision we have for our own communities. It is nothing new; these are values that have been treasured by the people of God for centuries, but when they are *all* embraced by one community, the results are extraordinary.

Our Father in heaven, hallowed be your name,
Your kingdom come, your will be done,
on earth as it is in heaven.

different

TO LEARN MORE ABOUT THE UNDERGROUND
AND GREENHOUSE MOVEMENTS, WATCH
AUTHOR INTERVIEWS, OR DOWNLOAD
A FREE DISCUSSION GUIDE, GO TO:

DIFFERENTBOOK.ORG

CHAPTER 1
1. Wiesel, Elie. Against Silence: the Voice and Vision of Elie Wiesel, Volume ii.
   New York: Holocaust Library, 1985.
2. Revelation 3:16.
3. 1 Peter 1:16.
4. 1 John 2:15-16.
5. Acts 5:13.
6. Acts 5:14.
7. 1 Peter 3:15.
8. 2 Corinthians 6:17-18.
9. 1 Peter 2:9. New King James Version.

CHAPTER 2
1. Tolstoy, Leo. Anna Karenina. (The Russian Messenger, 1877).
2. Douthat, Ross. Bad Religion: How We Became a Nation of Heretics (Free
   Press, 2013).
3. James Stewart, The Life and Teachings of Jesus Christ (New York, Abington
   Press, 1955). p. 207.
4. John 13:13-17.
5. 2 Corinthians 4:6.
6. Augustine, Saint. Homilies on the Gospel of John and on the First Epistle
   of John. Series 1, Volume 7. Philip Shaff, ed., Nicene and Post-Nicene
   Fathers. (William B. Eerdmans Publishing Company, 1956).
7. Hebrews 1:1-3.
8. Colossians 1:15-20.
9. Irenaeus. Against Heresies, Preface Book IV. (William B. Eerdmans
   Publishing Company, 2001).
10. Luke 4:18.
11. Isaiah 61:2.
12. 1 Corinthians 12:3.
13. Revelation 1:4-5.
14. Isaiah 53:7.

CHAPTER 3
1. Romans 12:1-2.
2. Ephesians 3:18.
3. Social proof: when people are uncertain about a course of action, they tend
   to look outside themselves and to other people around them to guide their
   decisions and actions, assuming that others know more about the situation.
4. John 15:17-19.
5. 1 Corinthians 2:2.

6. 1 Corinthians 1:2.
7. Cooley, Charles. The Looking Glass Self. (New York, C. Scribner's sons, 1902).
8. 1 John 3:1-3.
9. Philippians 1:6.
10. Matthew 18:21-35.
11. Ephesians 1:18

CHAPTER 4
1. Genesis 4:1.
2. Ephesians 5:32.
3. Matthew 16:17.
4. Psalm 25:14.
5. Psalm 25:15.
6. Revelation 2:4.
7. Psalm 27:4.
8. 2 Corinthians 3:18.
9. Matthew 6:6.
10. Matthew 6:5.
11. Matthew 6:6.
12. Genesis 3:8.
13. John 5:19.
14. Mark 1:35.
15. 2 Chronicles 26:5.
16. 2 Chronicles 26:15-16.

CHAPTER 5
1. Matthew 25:34-40.
2. John 15:12.
3. I John 3:16.
4. Benedicta Ward, The Sayings of the Desert Fathers: The Alphabetical Collection, (Cistercian Publications, 1975), 3.
5. Mark 8:29.
6. Mark 8:31.
7. 1 Corinthians 13:8.

CHAPTER 6
1. Matthew 11:11.
2. John 3:30.
3. Augustine, Saint. The Confessions of St. Augustine, (New York: Image Books, 1960).
4. Lewis, C.S. Mere Christianity. (New York: Macmillan Publishers, 1952).

5. Chesterton, Gilbert. Orthodoxy. (London: The Bodley Head, 1908).

6. Hunter, James. The Death of Character: Moral Education in an Age Without Good or Evil. (New York: Basic Books, 2001).

7. Luke 17:20.

8. Wagner, C Peter. Church Planting for a Greater Harvest: A Comprehensive Guide. (Ventura, Calif., U.S.A.: Regal Books, 1990).

9. Philippians 2:3-11.

10. Luke 22:24-31.

11. Greenleaf, Robert. Servant leadership: A journey into the nature of legitimate power and greatness. (New York: Paulist Press, 2002). P.24.

CHAPTER 7

1. John 15:8-12.

2. King, Martin Luther. Where Do We Go From Here? Delivered at 11th Annual SCLC Convention. Georgia, 1967.

3. Tillich, Paul. Love, Power, and Justice: Ontological Analysis and Ethical Applications. (Oxford and New York: Oxford University Press, 1954).

4. Tillich, Paul. Love, Power, and Justice: Ontological Analysis and Ethical Applications. (Oxford and New York: Oxford University Press, 1954).

5. John 10:18.

6. Song of Solomon 8:6.

7. Tillich, Paul. Love, Power, and Justice: Ontological Analysis and Ethical Applications. (Oxford and New York: Oxford University Press, 1954).

8. 2 Corinthians 10:3-4.

9. Kotter, John P. Leading Change. (Boston, Mass.: Harvard Business Review Press, 2012). P.

10. Proverbs 29:18.

11. Acts 2:17.

12. Matthew 28:16-20.

13. Matthew 16:20.

14. Matthew 28.18.

15. Revelation 4:2-4.

16. Matthew 20:25-26.

CHAPTER 8

1. Several studies bear this out. For a comprehensive argument see Author Brooks', "Who Really Cares: The Surprising Truth about Compassionate Conservatism," 2006.

2. 2 Corinthians 3:3.

3. James 2:14,17, emphasis ours.

4. James 1:3.

5. James 1:6.

6. James 2:1.
7. James 5:15.
8. John 3:16.
9. James 2:23.
10. James 2:18.
11. James 2:19.
12. James 2:20.
13. Acts 2:47.
14. James 2:21.
15. Ephesians 2:8-9.
16. 1 Peter 2:11-12.
17. Matthew 5:28.
18. Matthew 5:29.
19. 1 John 3:17.
20. Colossians 3:13.
21. James 2:1.
22. Proverbs 31:8-9.
23. James 5:16.
24. John 1:14.

CHAPTER 9
1. Mark 12:38-40.
2. Mark 12:41-44.
3. Mark 12:43-44.
4. Colossians 1:23.
5. Colossians 1:24.
6. Galations 5:6.

CHAPTER 10
1. 2 Peter 1:4.
2. Acts 1:4.
3. Acts 2:17.
4. Acts 4:31.
5. Acts 1:8.
6. Acts 8:8.
7. Acts 8:15-16.
8. John 16:7.
9. Galatians 4:6.
10. 2 Corinthians 1:21-22.
11. Ephesians 5:18.
12. 1 Corinthians 14:24-25.
13. I Corinthians 14:39.

14. Luke 11:9,13.
15. Genesis 1:26.

CHAPTER 11
1. Romans 10:14.
2. 1 Corinthians 9:16-18.
3. Matthew 11:7-9.
4. Toohey, Peter. Boredom: A Lively History (New Haven, Conn. Yale University Press, 2012).
5. Toohey, Peter. Boredom: A Lively History (New Haven, Conn. Yale University Press, 2012).
6. Matthew 7:28-29.
7. Matthew 9:33.
8. Matthew 15:31.
9. Matthew 8:27.
10. Mark 15:4.
11. Mark 15:5.
12. Acts 2:7-8.
13. Acts 2:12.
14. Romans 15:18.

CHAPTER 12
1. Matthew 28:18-20.
2. Ezekiel 34:4,6.
3. Philippians 3:17.
4. 2 Timothy 1:13.
5. 2 Timothy 3:10-11, emphasis ours.
6. Luke 9:18b.
7. Luke 9:20.
8. Luke 9:18a, emphasis ours.
9. Luke 6:12.
10. John 12:23-24.
11. 1 Samuel 2:12.
12. 1 Samuel 8:3.
13. 1 Samuel 2:25.